AF772802

The Legacy of William Schwartz: Group Practice as Shared Interaction

The *Social Work with Groups* series

Series Editors: Catherine P. Papell and Beulah Rothman

- *Co-Leadership in Social Work with Groups,* Catherine P. Papell and Beulah Rothman

- *Social Groupwork & Alcoholism,* Marjorie Altman and Ruth Crocker, Guest Editors

- *Groupwork with the Frail Elderly,* Shura Saul, Guest Editor

- *The Use of Group Services in Permanency Planning for Children,* Sylvia Morris, Guest Editor

- *Activities and Action in Groupwork,* Ruth Middleman, Guest Editor

- *Groupwork with Women/Groupwork with Men: An Overview of Gender Issues in Social Groupwork Practice,* Beth Glover Reed and Charles D. Garvin, Guest Editors

- *Ethnicity in Social Group Work Practice,* Larry Davis, Guest Editor

- *Time as a Factor in Groupwork,* Albert Alissi and Max Casper, Guest Editors

- *Groupwork with Children and Adolescents,* Ralph Kolodny and James Garland, Guest Editors

- *The Legacy of William Schwartz: Group Practice as Shared Interaction,* Alex Gitterman and Lawrence Shulman, Guest Editors

The Legacy of William Schwartz: Group Practice as Shared Interaction

Alex Gitterman and Lawrence Shulman
Guest Editors

The Haworth Press
New York • London

The Legacy of William Schwartz: Group Practice as Shared Interaction has also been published as *Social Work with Groups,* Volume 8, Number 4, Winter 1985/86.

© 1986 by The Haworth Press, Inc. All rights reserved. No part of this book may be reproduced or utilized in any form or by any means, electronic or mechanical, including photocopying, microfilm and recording, or by any information storage and retrieval system, without permission in writing from the publisher. Printed in the United States of America.

The Haworth Press, Inc., 28 East 22 Street, New York, NY 10010-6194
EUROSPAN/Haworth, 3 Henrietta Street, London, WC2E 8LU England

Library of Congress Cataloging in Publication Data
Main entry under title:

The Legacy of William Schwartz.

"Has also been published as Social work with groups, volume 8, number 4, winter 1985/86"—T.p. verso.
Includes bibliographies.
1. Social group work—Addresses, essays, lectures. 2. Social interaction—Addresses, essays, lectures. 3. Schwartz, William, 1916- . I. Gitterman, Alex, 1938- . II. Shulman, Lawrence.
HV45.L34 1986 361.4 85-17586
ISBN 0-86656-520-5

The Legacy of William Schwartz: Group Practice as Shared Interaction

Social Work with Groups
Volume 8, Number 4

CONTENTS

EDITORS

CATHERINE P. PAPELL, DSW, *Professor and Director, Direct Practice Division*
BEULAH ROTHMAN, DSW, *Professor Emeritus, Doctoral Program, Adelphi University School of Social Work, Garden City, Long Island, New York 11530*

EDITORIAL ASSOCIATES

URANIA E. GLASSMAN, MA, MSW, *Adelphi University School of Social Work*
BETH GUTTMAN, *Adelphi University School of Social Work*

AUDIO-VISUAL REVIEW EDITOR

LAWRENCE SHULMAN, EdD, *School of Social Work, University of British Columbia, Vancouver, Canada*

ADVISORY BOARD

PAUL ABELS, PhD, *School of Applied Social Services, Case Western Reserve University, Cleveland, Ohio*
ALBERT ALISSI, DSW, *University of Connecticut, School of Social Work, Greater Hartford Campus, West Hartford*
JOSEPH D. ANDERSON, DSW, *Social Welfare Department, Shippensburg State College, Shippensburg, Pennsylvania*
HARVEY BERTCHER, DSW, *School of Social Work, University of Michigan, Ann Arbor*
LEONARD N. BROWN, DSW, *Graduate School of Social Work, Rutgers State University*
MAX CASPER, MSW, *Syracuse University, School of Social Work*
LARRY DAVIS, PhD, *George Warren Brown School of Social Work, Washington University, St. Louis, Missouri*
MELVIN DELGADO, PhD, *School of Social Work, Boston University, Boston, Massachusetts*
HANS S. FALCK, PhD, *School of Social Work and Medical College of Virginia Commonwealth University, Richmond*
RONALD A. FELDMAN, PhD, *George Warren Brown School of Social Work, Washington University, St. Louis, Missouri*
LOUISE A. FREY, MS, *Boston University School of Social Work*
MAEDA J. GALINSKY, PhD, *School of Social Work, University of North Carolina, Chapel Hill*
JAMES GARLAND, MSSS, *Boston University School of Social Work*
CHARLES GARVIN, PhD, *School of Social Work, University of Michigan, Ann Arbor*
GEORGE GETZEL, DSW, *School of Social Work, Hunter College of the City University of New York*
ALEX GITTERMAN, EdD, *Columbia University School of Social Work, New York*
PAUL H. GLASSER, PhD, *University of Texas at Arlington School of Social Work*
MARGARET E. HARTFORD, PhD, *Leonard Davis School of Gerontology, University of Southern California, Los Angeles*
SUE HENRY, DSW, *Graduate School of Social Work, University of Denver*
ALAN F. KLEIN, MSW, JD, *School of Social Welfare, State University of New York at Albany*
RALPH L. KOLODNY, MSSS, *Boston University School of Social Work*

GISELA KONOPKA, DSW, *Center for Youth Development and Research, University of Minnesota, St. Paul*
NORMA C. LANG, PhD, *Faculty of Social Work, University of Toronto*
JUDITH B. LEE, DSW, *School of Social Work, University of Connecticut*
BARUCH LEVINE, PhD, *Jane Addams College of Social Work, University of Illinois, and private practice, Chicago*
HENRY W. MAIER, PhD, *School of Social Work, University of Washington, Seattle*
RUTH R. MIDDLEMAN, EdD, *Raymond A. Kent School of Social Work, University of Louisville, Kentucky*
HELEN NORTHEN, PhD, *School of Social Work, University of Southern California, Los Angeles*
RUBY B. PERNELL, DSW, *School of Applied Social Sciences, Case Western Reserve University, Cleveland*
HELEN PHILLIPS, DSW, *School of Social Work, University of Pennsylvania, Philadelphia*
HERMAN RESNICK, PhD, *School of Social Work, University of Washington, Seattle*
SHELDON ROSE, PhD, *School of Social Work, University of Wisconsin, Madison*
JANICE H. SCHOPLER, MSW, *School of Social Work, University of North Carolina, Chapel Hill*
MARY LOUISE SOMERS, DSW, *School of Social Service Administration, University of Chicago*
RON TOSELAND, PhD, *University of New York at Albany, New York*
EMANUEL TROPP, MSSW, *School of Social Work, Virginia Commonwealth University, Richmond*
ROBERT VINTER, PhD, *School of Social Work, University of Michigan, Ann Arbor*
CELIA B. WEISMAN, DSW, *Wurzweiler School of Social Work, Yeshiva University, New York*

EDITORIAL

This special issue of *Social Work with Groups* was born out of our sense that practitioners, educators and students, present and future, would wish to memorialize someone who participated so richly in the development of social group work theory. Not only is the legacy of William Schwartz a gift to those who personally experienced him as a teacher or colleague but to all social workers. His writings have been a significant center-piece in the literature of a group work spanning the golden age of the 50's and the resurgence of interest in group work practice in the 80's. The vitality of his ideas has served as a spring board for the continuing examination of the complex action and helping processes that occur in the group.

William Schwartz introduced and elaborated for group work a preeminent theme, namely mutual aid. While other theoreticians, prior to Schwartz and after, recognized the mutual helping processes in groups, it was Schwartz who gave it a primacy which brought direction and focus to social group work practice in relation to the group as a unit of service. The identity of group work in the profession became increasingly tied to this concept, distinguishing social work practice with groups from other group helping methods. Around this theme role relationships and operational principles for the worker were developed and continue to be refined for social work practice with groups.

William Schwartz was a savant before his time. His sophisticated, imaginative understanding of system and interdependence opened the way for social group workers to work more directly, less self-

© 1986 by The Haworth Press, Inc. All rights reserved.

consciously, and more appreciatively of the members' strengths and purposes. His concept of the mediating role for the social group worker is drawn from his profound understanding of systemic interdependence in any human situation. His writings, from this philosophical stance, integrated the essential interdependence of the individual and society which he recognized as expressed in a primary way in the group.

The career of Schwartz as a social group worker began at an interesting time in the history of our profession when the struggle between the functional and dynamic schools represented a troubling cleavage. His independence and creativity as a group practitioner and theoretician led him to search both approaches for what was organismically relevant to his fundamental view of social work. His unconstrained and inductive mode of thought led him to reject the medically oriented "diagnosis" of the psychoanalytic model and similarly to reject the unconditional professional authoritativeness of the functional model. He held firmly to casting social work as a dynamic process with an outcome determined by the interdependent needs and interaction of groups members and worker in the context of the agency. Schwartz bridged both approaches in his writings and served a valuable linkage function for group work. This was later extended in his faculty years at Columbia. He was a part of the movement in the profession to create varied theoretical models for examining practice without loss of the essence of the helping commitment.

Schwartz was a distinguished representative of group work in the profession of social work. The clarity and eloquence with which he expressed his thoughts and ideas about social work, the profundity and existential nature of his understanding and his command of wit and ethnic humor made it possible for him to debate and collaborate with the leadership of the profession and thus to advance the stature and awareness of the group methodology. His untiring quest for operationalized principles that would guide the group worker's action spurred the theoretical development and conceptualizing of methodology and technique. His influence in this regard can best be ascertained in the frequency with which his principles of practice are referenced as direct or derivative resources in the articles of this journal and throughout the literature of the profession.

We were privileged to know William Schwartz throughout his professional career. He influenced us as he did others. However, the strength of his ideas transcends time and personal contact. Group work was indeed fortunate to have had such a giant. Like all giants his opinions were powerful, his demands of self and others high, his insights compelling.

Our two guest editors, Alex Gitterman and Lawrence Shulman, his wife, Ruth Schwartz, and the other contributors to this issue, whose professional works are animated by his ideas, exemplify the transcendence of the legacy of William Schwartz. We are all indebted.

C.P.
B.R.

GUEST EDITORIAL

This issue is in tribute to the lasting contribution of William Schwartz to teaching and scholarship. Bill was a man of ideas who broke with traditional formulations and established a heuristic paradigm. He expressed his ideas with eloquent simplicity and uncommon clarity, disdaining academic and professional jargon. His articles introduced new and exciting propositions about social work function, mutual-aid, professional method, and contract. These have had a powerful impact upon professional practice and education.

The Journal begins with a historical presentation by Bill. He traces with characteristic clarity and style the development of social work with groups. Gitterman examines and evaluates Schwartz's contribution to social work knowledge and practice. These are followed by Lee who describes the value of an integrative practice perspective, using Schwartz's Reciprocal Model and Germain's and Gitterman's Life Model to frame her discussion. Shulman examines the concept of mutual aid, capturing its subtleties and practice applications. And Shields applies Bill's ideas to an adolescent school group. These articles attempt to convey the power of Bill's ideas and their relevance for contemporary practice.

As teacher, Bill challenged his students to think for themselves. He invited them to participate in an educational journey, helping them to experience intellectually and emotionally the subject being studied. Integrating theory and practice was the desired outcome. And for this integration to take place, Bill invited, cajoled and demanded his students simultaneously to personalize and experience

© 1986 by The Haworth Press, Inc. All rights reserved.

theoretical formulations as well as to conceptualize and pattern practice experiences. Through his teaching artistry, students were exposed to remarkable breakthroughs and discoveries about the subject and themselves and the most difficult task of all, their integration. Phillips and Weber describe and illustrate Bill's ideas in the classroom. They participated in a pedagogical seminar he led and apply his ideas to their teaching. Robertson and Ginsberg, former students, describe a teaching instrument used by Bill, the Log, in helping students actively to search for the connections between the "abstract" and "real worlds."

We are honored to edit this collection and hope it does justice to its purpose.

Alex Gitterman
Lawrence Shulman

The Group Work Tradition and Social Work Practice

William Schwartz

The social work profession is one of the primary institutions designed to help people negotiate the complicated systems in which they live. Its efforts have followed three major impulses. The most prominent of these has been to deal with people individually, "case by case," seeking to remedy the psychological and social conditions that have brought their problems about. Theories of responsibility vary with the times—individual and social, moral, economic, and psychological—but in most instances those who seek help are seen as somehow personally inadequate, and the effort is made to render them more self-sufficient, psychologically stronger, less dependent on help from the outside. The worker-client relationship is intimate, confidential, and takes place on the professional's own ground. The client is carefully examined, and the condition "diagnosed"—in the adopted medical language—as a prelude to "treatment." The rationale for this thorough personal inquiry is today largely scientific, following the medical approach to illness. But the tradition goes back a long way. Thomas Chalmers, an early precursor of the Charity Organization movement, said of those who came to seek economic assistance: "He who seeks another's bounty shall also submit to another's scrutiny."[1] This one-on-one approach to human problems is the discipline we have called social casework, and it has been the dominant feature of the social work profession since its inception.

A second direction has been to help needy people in their own milieux, surrounded by their peers and working in an atmosphere of mutual aid. Here the effort is to find, in the people's own conditions of life, the energy and the resources with which they can help each

This paper was presented at the 25th Anniversary Symposia, Graduate School of Social Work, Rutgers, the State University of New Jersey, and is republished with permission from *Social Work Futures: Essays Commemorating Twenty-Five Years of the Graduate School of Social Work,* Edited by Miriam Dinerman, published by the Graduate School of Social Work, Rutgers, The State University of New Jersey in cooperation with the Council on Social Work Education, 1983, New Brunswick, NJ.

other act together on common problems. People are brought together for many reasons: to organize themselves for action on special interests and common concerns; to help each other face difficult personal problems; to learn new skills with which to enrich the quality of their lives. The setting is the small, face-to-face group, placed in some shared community context; experiences are communicated among the members, rather than held confidential between member and worker; and the worker is surrounded by a host of surrogate helpers, each claiming a share of the supportive function. The lines of communication are intricate, and the worker's authority is diffused in the network of relationships that goes to make up the pattern of mutual aid. This is the direction we came to know as social group work, and it has grown over the years to occupy an increasingly significant place in the work of the profession.

The third approach has been to deal with the social problems themselves, rather than the people who suffer under their effects. The lines between direct service and social planning have not always been distinct, nor has it been necessary that they be so. In fact, both the early settlements and the Charity Organization movement were prime examples of the integration of direct practice and what we now call community organization and social reform. But the deepening troubles of industrial capitalism, and the accompanying complexities administering social welfare, created this specialized field, with its own knowledge and skills, that addressed itself to the tasks of social and legislative action, the development and distribution of resources, intergroup cooperation, and—maintaining its ties to direct service—the organization of grass-roots action on community problems.

The history of social work is the story of how these different ways of helping people in need came together to find a single professional identity. In 1873, the National Conference of Charities and Correction first offered the humanitarians a chance to share their common aspirations and working problems.[2] In the 1920's, the Milford Conference found some theoretical unity for social casework, at a time when that was considered tantamount to integrating the entire profession.[3] And in the 1950's, the National Association of Social Workers was born of a long organizational process that merged seven independent social work organizations into a single association that represented social workers of America who had formal educational preparation.[4,5]

The search for a common identity for social work did not end when this union was effected. Today, a generation later, it still remains to find the common technology that could render its practitioners recognizable as part of a single professional entity. It has been relatively easy to describe the common objectives, the shared values, even the relevant areas of knowledge; but it has been much more difficult to define the basic skills that bind them together and constitute a special claim to conpetence in serving the community. Parsons, in his study of the legal profession, defined the professional as a "technical expert . . . by virtue of his mastery of the tradition and skills of its use."[6] How would such a principle be applied to social work? What is its common tradition, and to what special skills does it lay its claim? What abilities do the family worker, the camp director, the organizer, the club leader, the clinician-therapist have in common? Are they in any measure interchangeable, considering that they all hold the same graduate degree?

It is, of course, the old search for the generic, in a jungle of specifics. The merger of professional associations, however desirable it may have been, left yet to be done the task of merging the separate experiences and histories of social work into a commonly understood way of working with people. Although structurally unified, the profession is still more like a coalition of the old "methods" than it is an integrated discipline combining the richest and most effective elements of each.

It is true that such development does not happen overnight; the Milford Conference, for example, took close to a decade to sort out the generic and the specific in social casework. In our own generation, we have had some thoughtful work on the subject,[7,8] and there will be more. But I believe that such an effort would be considerably advanced if each of the so-called "methods" were to explore its own traditions of practice to find those unique elements that might help to put its own special stamp on a unified conception of the function and practice of social work. My effort here is to examine something of the group work heritage, looking back on some of its early history, its theoretical underpinnings, its conception of the client, the worker-member relationship, and its conduct of the helping process. In a short paper, one can only touch on the main themes; but I would hope to give some of the flavor of such an enterprise, and stimulate others to work along similar lines.[9]

The Early Years

There is a common misconception that group work is considerably younger than its casework sibling. In fact, the ancestors of both movements began their work at about the same time in history, with the group work agencies following the casework establishments by only a few years. Canon Barnett, the founder of the first settlement—Toynbee Hall in London—was a close associate of Octavia Hill, who played a similar role in the beginnings of the London Charity Organization Society; Barnett was in fact influential in both movements.[10] In this country, Jane Addams and Mary Richmond were colleagues and very much aware that they were part of a common enterprise. Both in England and in the United States, the settlements and the Societies were not far apart: the London COS in 1868, Toynbee Hall in 1884, the Buffalo COS in 1877, Jane Addams's Hull-House in 1889. As to the seminal works in both fields, Mary Richmond's *Social Diagnosis* was issued in 1917,[11] while Grace Coyle's *Social Process in Organized Groups* came in 1930.[12] In general, the early workers were all part of the same group of social reformers that came out of the Progressive Era. Their motives were much the same, and they knew and worked with each other long before the casework-group work distinctions were drawn. Canon Barnett's favored motto—embroidered and hung in his drawing room in Whitechapel—was "One By One."[13]

The historical difference between the two movements was that casework, or individual work, became almost immediately synonymous with social work as its practitioners sprang into action, defined themselves as a body, formed a national conference, began to systematize their thinking,[14] and produced a steady stream of writing about their experiences in the field. The group workers, on the other hand, were much more diverse in their outlook, identifying themselves with many fields of endeavor, among them education, recreation, camping, and mental hygiene—each with a tradition of its own going back to 1861[15]—as well as social work. The American Association for the Study of Group Work, founded in 1936, numbered among its members people from all these professions, as well as those with purely academic and scientific interest in the small group, without any particular reference to its professional uses.

This wide range of interests and allegiances was reflected in a study of the leisure-time agencies in the 1920's, which concluded that "the objectives of these various agencies would at first thought seem so divergent as to make it impossible to treat the duties and responsibilities of their workers in the same analysis."[16]

Group work's ambivalence about where it belonged continued even after its place was established, both in social work education and as part of the National Conference of Social Work, in the mid-'30s. In 1940, the noted educator William Heard Kilpatrick asserted that "this group work is . . . not to be thought of as a separate field of work, but rather as a method to be used in all kinds of educational effort."[17] And as late as 1946, we find Grace Coyle herself still concerned about the "alignment" of group workers: "One baffling problem has plagued the development of professional consciousness among group workers over this decade. It is usually phrased in terms of alignment, and a dilemma is presented. We must, it seems, be either educators or social workers."[18]

Ultimately, the choice was made, and group work practitioners found their place within the social work profession. It was, after all, group work's natural habitat, having had its origins in the humanitarian movement and its major development within the agencies of social welfare.

> Social work, with its early emphasis on the individual in his environment, was a congenial host for those whose work lay at the very point of interaction between the two. Social work's concern with the total individual, the importance of community life, and the role of government in human affairs offered a comfortable resting place for group work's unique blend of scientific, humanitarian, and missionary zeal. . . .[19]

It was at that point that the question changed from whether group workers would identify themselves as social workers to what they would bring with them into a unified field of practice. Undoubtedly, there was much in their world view that was the same as that of the other approaches within the profession. But there must also be, from the settings and circumstances of their encounters with human beings in need, a great deal that was different, through which group work could make a valuable contribution to a generic conception of the work of the profession. To find these, one would have to look closely at several key areas in their collective early experience.

Group Work Purposes

If the caseworkers were the "priests" of social welfare, and the social planners were its "prophets," the group workers were a kind of cross between the two.[20] On the one hand, they were deeply involved in direct service to the poor, ministering to their needs in day-to-day contact; on the other, because they worked where the people lived, they were first-hand witnesses to the cramped quality of the people's lives and the limitations of a political and economic system in which huge sections of the population were neglected, uninvolved, and relegated to the fringes of power. Catherine Cooke Gilman suggested that the motto of the settlements might be: "Keep your fingers on the near things and eyes on the far things."[21]

These were the twin emphases that pervaded the work of the first agencies—the "near things" of individual need and the "far things" of social reform. On the one hand, the early settlement papers were replete with references to "self": self-development, self-sufficiency, self-respect, and the like.[22] At the same time, there was a strong preoccupation with the need for education for political power. "If power is to be dispersed, then everybody is to be trained to exercise it. . . . Democracy becomes a farce, not because it has lost its ideal force but because its devotees are, democratically speaking, illiterate; they do not know how to operate in and through groups."[23]

In order to provide a new version of society, a community in which people could regain some control over their immediate environment, the early workers turned to the small group as a context for action. This connection between individual and social strength may seem naive to us today, but it appeared to the settlement pioneers to be compelling; they had an enormous faith in human association, and the small group was to be an instrument of personal growth as well as what they called a "building block of democracy." Jane Addams spoke of exchanging "the music of isolated voices [for] the volume and strength of the chorus."[24] And Canon Barnett said: ". . . if it be a great matter to be an individual, it is a greater matter to be part of a whole . . ."[25]

Underlying all of these purposes, there lay the urge to restore to the people those aspects of life that had been denied to them by the ravages of industrialization. The crowded city streets, the dearth of recreational opportunities, the absence of trees and country spaces, the lack of time for play—all of these produced a great yearning for space, country, and leisure. It was the need that spawned Barnett's Children's Country Holiday Fund in England, and vitalized the camping and playground movements in this country. The group work pioneers waxed particularly eloquent on the subject of play. "A people's play," said Mrs. Henrietta Barnett, "is a fair test of a people's character. Their recreation more than their business or their conquests settle the nations' place in history.''[26] And consider this paean to its virtues:

> Play has physical, psychological, social, ethical, and spiritual significance. . . . Play is joy-producing and hence develops mental optimism. Play naturally and unconsciously places the individual in right relations with his social group. Play is the testing-laboratory of the individual and the social virtues. Play rounds out our fragmentary lives and makes us spiritually whole.[27]

This concern with enhancing the quality of life was at the heart of the preoccupation with cultural activities—music, art, literature, drama, trips, discussion—as well as occasions, entertainments, and general atmosphere of intimate and informal exchange. Barnett claimed that his ultimate resource was his wife's tea-table.[28] The themes of informality, social intercourse, shared experience, and, above all, friendship, were at the very roots of the settlement movement. Friendship was the bond that would unite them all—the residents and the neighbors, workers and members. Indeed friendship was to be a political instrument. The young, well-favored, well-to-do students who came to the first university settlements—of which Toynbee Hall was one—were being trained to rule more wisely by making real friendships with the poor and learning at first hand their way of life. The class struggle was in their eyes a product of misunderstanding between the rich and the poor, and it could be mitigated by working out these failures of communication on the people's home ground. ''The classes are out of joint,'' wrote Barnett ''and do not work together to one end. The call is still for a way of peace, and for a means of promoting good fellowship between man and man.''[29]

And so group work came to the people with an active agenda and a sackful of hopes and prayers for individual salvation and social change. Although Barnett himself went to some pains to point out that settlements are not missions, and should not be used for ''doing good,'' or for preaching a message,[30] the total effect over the years has been to invest the worker-client engagement with urgent conviction and well-marked educational purposes. Later, when ''cause'' began to edge its way toward ''function,'' there would be considerable difficulty in distinguishing means from ends. But there was rarely any danger that the group workers would go passive, or neutral, about what the world should be like. They would carry their strong sense of the individual-social connections with them into the social work arena. It was a heavy load, and they often carried it clumsily; but always the worker was an active and intimate participant in the client's experience.

It was a new kind of relationship, this collaboration between a worker and the members of a group, and it raised questions that went beyond the Freudian explanations that were being studied so intently by the rest of the profession. Unbound as they were to any one field of exploration, they had a whole world to turn to; and they did—to the educators, the sociologists, the psychologists, and the host of disciplines that were exploding with new insights at the turn of the 20th century.

Theoretical Foundations

The intellectual renaissance that took place in America as part of the Progressive Era was in many ways responsive to the needs and curiosities of the group work movement. New knowledge came from many directions—religious, philosophical, social, psychological, political— and the group workers, not yet tied to any hard-and-fast identifications, were free to look where they chose for enlightenment and inspiration. The Freudian answers found some ready group work adherents, as they did in casework, but the fit was uncomfortable, the explanations skirting many of the situational questions raised by the group experience. It was not that the group workers had no interest in personality development; obviously they must have. But their point of vantage led them to observe human behavior in its social, relational context. Their curiousities were essentially what we would now call *systemic,* having to do with interrelational networks; and their questions were oriented to issues of action and interaction, the nature of shared experience, and the processes of communication—verbal and nonverbal—within the small group.

Their field of inquiry was broad, and it would take a much longer work than this to trace the precise connections between the growing body of early 20th century knowledge and the development of group work thinking. But certain influences are fairly clear, and important to our present purpose. The great progenitor of small-group analysis was, of course, Charles Horton Cooley, whose researches into the nature of the primary group provided a profound rationale for the social uses of human togetherness. It was Cooley who took his stand against the opposition of self and society, uniting these into a single, unified concept. He said: "By primary groups I mean those characterized by intimate face-to-face association and cooperation. They are primary in several senses, but chiefly in that they are fundamental in forming the social nature and ideals of the individual."[31] It was a radical idea, and it explained much of the group workers' experience with people. ". . . human nature is not something existing separately in the individual, but a *group-nature* . . ."[32] And he echoed another part of their experience as he described the feeling of "we": "one lives in the feeling of the whole and finds the chief aims of his will in that feeling."[33]

The concept of the social nature of human personality was a landmark in our intellectual history, and it was highly congenial to those who worked in the context of community. The group workers turned to others with the same idea—Baldwin,[34] Kropotkin,[35] and Dewey[36] in the early years, and later Mead,[37] Sherif, [38] Lewin,[39] and the host of others that followed. The implications of this insight moved directly to the heart of one of the great issues of group work practice, namely the persistent tendency to dichotomize the needs of individuals and those of the collective. Baldwin put it this way:

> It is, to my mind, the most remarkable outcome of modern social theory—the recognition of the fact that the individual's normal growth lands him in essential solidarity with his fellows, while on the other hand the exercise of his social duties and privileges advances his highest and purest individuality.[40]

Like all great insights, this one raised new questions to replace those it answered. How, for example, did one understand the processes of interaction between people who were not fixed entities but social creations, the ever-changing products of those same interactions? For this they turned to Mary Follett, an ex-settlement worker in working-class Boston, who wrote books analyzing the group experience, the uses of authority, the nature of freedom, and similar, eagerly debated, issues affecting group work practice. Her concept of "circular behavior" emphasized the *reverberating* character of human exchanges, in which each actor responds to a situation he helped create a moment ago. She pointed out that "response is always to a relation. I respond, not only to you, but to the relation between you and me."[41] This idea took on considerable meaning as workers tried to describe a helping process in which they did not attempt to change the fixed and immutable "personality" of their members, but viewed both client and worker as in a continuing process of shifting and changing under the moment-by-moment impact of each upon the other. In the spontaneous, ever-active ambience of the group experience, this latter version, however difficult to describe, was felt to be closer to experience than the subject-object, "change-agent," what Buber was later to call the "I-It" rather than the "I-Thou"[42] version of the helping process.

It was a day-by-day discovery of the group workers that communication was only partly a formal, verbal affair, and that much of the human exchange could be read in the language of action—in games, body language, and expressive play. In this area, their teacher was Neva Leona Boyd. Using her long experience as a pioneer of the recreation movement, and taking her cues from the literature of spontaneity and progressive education, she asserted that "the only morality there is is bound up with action."[43] She urged the group workers to free themselves "from the limitations imposed by an overemphasis on verbalized aspects of expression."[44] And she said: "Only in the spontaneous, uncalculated response of human beings to each other can sensitivity to undefined subtleties function."[45]

There was a great deal more, and as the field moved into the '30s and '40s, it was Grace Coyle and her colleagues who pulled it all together and made it into a syllabus. The time for building their own theoretical base was getting short; there would be less than ten years between the formation of the American Association of Group Workers in 1946 and its merger into the National Association of Social Workers in 1955, and there were many important questions left to be resolved.

The Group Work Client

There are those who claim that all of social work is a kind of "battlefield medicine," in which the object is to patch up the victims as best one can and put them back in the field as soon as possible. If this is so, then the triage was arranged so that the group workers took those who were the less incapacitated and somewhat more capable of conducting their affairs as part of a small community. This is not to say, as it is so often, that their people were "normal"—there are so few of those around—but simply that they had enough energy to engage themselves with others in common tasks.

The emphasis was on working with strengths, rather than curing illness. At the 1935 National Conference of Social Work, LeRoy Bowman said: "Group work . . . is not a service to those who ask for help—it is the social mechanism perfectly competent people utilize to achieve their own ends."[46] And just as Virginia Robinson had written that "one does not go to a [casework] agency joyfully,"[47] Grace Coyle stresses the "true enjoyment [that] comes when the self is . . . actively and vitally engaged, its powers expanding in fulfillment."[48]

Thus it was that the very concept of "client" was somewhat strange, even distasteful, for many group workers, preferring as they did the designation of "member." Bowman was careful to make a point of this at the same conference in 1935, asserting that group workers "must help to relate the members of their groups (I did not say 'clients') to the national or mass concerns of the day."[49] The argument about terms was, of course, part of the aforementioned ambivalence about social work itself; but it had a deeper significance in that the "member" orientation helped bring millions of new middle-class consumers into group work's field of action, as the group work skills were sought out by the youth movements, community centers, "Y"s, and Jewish Centers that were coming into being all over the country.

The distinction between "client" and "member" was not always easy to maintain; group workers were constantly dealing with group members who were struggling under a heavy load of personal problems as they tried to meet the demand for responsible group participation. Thus workers faced what came increasingly to feel like a choice between their concern for individuals in trouble and their aspirations for the group as a whole. Here again was the self-society dilemma in its practice manifestation: whether to get on with the collective tasks or to stop for those who needed help in catching up with the others. The "choice," though it was much discussed, always turned out to be an illusion, in the small group as in the larger community: when one "chose" the individual and abandoned the others, the group foundered and all suffered; and when the worker addressed himself exclusively to the collective, ignoring those who needed special help, there was a mounting residue of anger and guilt, felt by both members and worker.

Out of this dilemma there emerged what has been called the "two clients" conception, in which the worker's function is to help both the individual and the group, the one to meet his needs within the system, the other to pursue its collective tasks. The value of this idea was that it called for considerable skill and forced the worker to try to unify his responsibility for both the individual and the group, instead of hovering indecisively between the two, always worrying about whether he should be sacrificing one for the other.

But the trouble with the "two clients" idea was that it was still dualistic in nature. While "both" was superior to "either-or," it was really only a different version of it, and it tended to produce a kind of pseudo-solution that obscured a deeper insight into the problem. What was needed was a closer look at the working relationship between a person and his group, to find the common need, the common ground, the common impetus that carried them toward each other.[50] In this view, the worker's function was to act as a bridge across which the individual could reach out to negotiate the system of demands and opportunities offered by his group, while at the same time helping the collective reach out to incorporate each of its members in the group life.[51] The worker would thus define his "client"—or his major responsibility—as neither the individual nor the group, but the *processes* that passed between them. The group workers had learned about process from Dewey, Follett, Lindeman, and others; it was a natural outgrowth of their interest in social action and social experience. It was no accident that Coyle's first landmark publication was called *Social Process in Organized Groups,* while Mary Richmond's was entitled *Social Diagnosis*.

The group workers could not always muster the skills necessary to help carry people and their significant groups toward each other; the burden of process is not easy to carry in a product-oriented society. Nevertheless, operating where these problems were always right before their eyes, they could not but form the habit of viewing people in their social context. When they looked at an individual—be he "client" or "member"—they could not fail to see him as surrounded by his culture, his family, and his friends.

The Worker-Client Relationship

The earliest conception of the helping relationship in group work was of one that took place within a community of equals. As I have indicated, the theme of friendship was paramount in the minds of the founders: "Charity is friendship," said Canon Barnett, "and. . . institutions which don't give friends are not charity."[52] The Charity Organization Society also used the slogan "not alms but a friend,"[53] but the settlements used the term literally, and carried it into action with its daily opportunities for physical contact, joint action, group entertainments, and the like.

The theme of camaraderie—of comradeship as an instrument of helping—had a lasting effect on the development of the group work tradition. It became a subject of humor in the sophisticated fellowship into which it subsequently entered, but when the idea of friendship was later transformed into that of leadership, the group workers found themselves formulating an important problem in the uses of professional authority. How did one maintain an active, intimate, spontaneous relationship with a person in need, while yet retaining the distance and discipline necessary to carry out a professional function? How did a worker act freely without acting out?

Freud's discovery of the "transference" in the doctor-patient relationship[54] was a revelation to workers in the helping disciplines, and it was eagerly taken up by the newly emerging social work profession. He had written that "eventually all the conflicts must be fought out on the field of transference,"[55] and, in advising physicians on the use of the psychoanalytic method, he had laid great stress on the absolute "impenetrability" of the doctor in the face of this phenomenon:

> The loosening of the transference, too—one of the main tasks of the cure—is made more difficult by too intimate an attitude on the part of the doctor, so that a doubtful gain in the beginning is more than cancelled in the end. Therefore I do not hesitate to condemn this kind of technique as incorrect. The physician should be impenetrable to the patient, and, like a mirror, reflect nothing but what is shown to him.[56]

Obviously, such a doctrine, however useful in helping workers understand more deeply the meaning of professional authority, was difficult to apply directly in the hustle-bustle of the group experience. And, as we might expect, there was some horror at the prospect. Again it was Bowman who stated the problem:

> Any good group worker knows, as does any good progressive teacher, that such a relationship is the opposite of that desired by the group leader. It is not transference to the leader at all, but cross transference between the members, that should form the dynamic influence in group activities.[57]

In this area as in others, the group workers found the new, system-oriented ideas more congenial to their experience. While always troubled by their tendency towards counter-transference, and their vulnerability to its effects, it was difficult to remain "impenetrable" in a game of steal-the-bacon, or a trip to a strange place, or a discussion of serious group problems. But they could echo to Follett's description of the helping relationship as circular and reciprocal—"a reaction to a relating." And they could respond to her brilliant insight, realized as early as the '20s, that leadership was not essentially a factor of personality—what she called "ascendency traits"—but a functional, situational manifestation. "Don't exploit your personality," she said to them. "*Learn your job.*"[58]

Later in their development, the group workers would be heavily influenced by Grace Coyle's distillation of the educational process and her conception of the *mentoring* and *modelling* aspects of the professional relationship.

> In this interacting mesh of life, whatever the content of program, teaching and learning are a mutual process. If the leader is himself achieving his own guiding values, his own delight in excellence, his own deep sense of the validity and meaning of life, his own ability to function as part of the social whole, that achieving by a kind of delicate osmosis is likely to be his most significant contribution to his group.[59]

Thus the traditional worker-member relationship in group work was that of a co-active, reciprocal, functional, first-among-equals, mentoring collaboration in the pursuit of group tasks. What kind of helping process was it that emerged from all this?

On the Nature of Helping

The legacy of group work, like that of many of the helping professions, lies more in its accumulated experience and its sense of social purpose than in its understanding of its own technical skills. Towley commented on this at about the time when group work was merging its identity with that of the social work profession:

> This specialized field is rich in democratic concepts; it has a wealth of examples; but in professionally unique concepts, "method theory," it has been curiously poor. . . . It is possi-

> ble that no social or economic class in a community is beyond profiting from what goes on under the name of a "group experience." But it is difficult for a social group worker to communicate how and why this near-miracle happens, except to another group worker.[60]

It was true; but from their "wealth of examples"—that is, the social history of their experiences with people—it is possible to bring into clearer focus some of the action implications of what the group workers thought about their purpose, knowledge, professional relationships, and the rest. Given these conceptions, and given the demands of the settings in which they worked, they were compelled to fashion certain kinds of working skills. Whether or not they were always equal to these demands—early records leave some doubts on that score—the group workers nevertheless developed certain perspectives on the helping process that were unique to their calling.

First, since the worker found himself located inside the group members' sphere of activity—a part of their play, their talk, and their transactions—his comments had to be made not as a detached observer and interpreter but as an active participant with his own functional stake in the proceedings. The concept of "intervention," although it would later become fashionable, was essentially inappropriate since one does not "intervene" in a system from the inside; it is a contradiction in terms. Within the system, the worker's function was to provide the skills with which to mediate the transactions between each individual and the group, reinforcing the energies with which they reached out to each other. In this position, two major, concurrent tasks are faced: on the one hand, to help each member come to grips with the worker's authority and use it to the member's own advantage; while at the same time, to help members use each other in the collective effort. Later, Bennis and Shepard and others would teach them more about these processes of *authority* and *intimacy,* how they operated, and the connections between the two.[61] But whether or not they understood exactly what was happening, group workers' skills were fashioned by such demands, as were their conceptions of the helping process in action.

Second, since the workings of groups made them often restless and mobile, group work skills were at the outset less tuned to introspection and the pursuit of insight than to the advancement of action. Their early interest in non-verbal, extra-logical forms of communication had helped them develop proficiency in many of the expressive phenomena—phantasy, play, drama, music, travelling, and the rest; it is only recently that formal courses in these "program" subjects have been dropped from the graduate school curricula. What remains, however, is the sensitivity to the language of action, and the awareness that talk and action are not antithetical, the former serious and the latter trivial and distracting, but different, often simultaneous, aspects of the communication between worker and clients.

Third, it was not possible for the worker to maintain an orderly and logical progression of ideas when constantly being called upon to react quickly in the press of events. The agenda was often controlled by impulse and feeling, and the worker had to develop the ability to make quick connections and find underlying themes, protecting professional purposes even while moving spontaneously into the action. The sight of a worker sitting wrapped in thought while those around him were feeling and acting was not calculated to inspire confidence in the interest and empathy of professional help. It was not possible for a worker successfully to urge freedom and openness on one's members while serving as a model of caution and circumspection. It called for considerable risking on the worker's part; but risking, after all, was a major ingredient in the client's prescription, and it was a poor sort of authority that gave the message to the client to "do as I say, not as I do."

Finally, since the members' main source of enjoyment and profit came from their ability to show their strengths with others, the group workers had to develop the skills with which to help the members find those strengths and use them in the group. The workers' efforts were primitive at first, relying heavily on urging and exhortation. Later, taught by Alfred Adler, Carl Rogers, and the ego psychologists, they fashioned more sophisticated techniques to mobilize client strength: partializing difficult issues; reaching for real feelings; using role-playing to help translate feelings into action; turning members toward each other for support and reality-testing; reaching for ideas that were hard to express publicly; and connecting private troubles with group concerns.

One could explore many more aspects of the group work gestalt that emerged from the need to do a helping job within a setting that, because it was social, public, and on the clients' home ground, made unusual demands upon the worker. This is not to say that the helping process in group work was *sui generis,* or totally different from other approaches; indeed the point of this paper is that it was only a special manifestation of social work in action. But, over and above the similarities, group work's special character lay in the fact that its experience brought into focus certain phenomena that are less easily seen when the work is private, one-on-one, and under the worker's almost total control.

Toward an Expanded Paradigm

The old settlement idea of the helping relationship as a shared experience meant that residents and neighbors, workers and group members, were on a voyage of discovery, affecting each other's lives, tied together with a common bond, fulfilling each one's own special purposes in the process. The idea was drawn from the very air of Victorian society; it was class-dominated, idealistic, and amateurish in many ways. But its deeper truth lay in its vision of a relationship in which the qualities of leadership were expressed in the joys of human collaboration, rather than in the action of the knower on the naive, the strong on the weak, the expert on the uninitiated. As I have indicated, the intimacy of worker and members created the need to guard one's function carefully, lest it be lost in the close exchange. But the opposite view—detached, "objective," and often identified as more *truly* professional—raises a more serious problem; the distance between worker and client is then so large, and the worker's position on the periphery of the system so secure, that there is no longer any risk at all, and the worker is too safe to worry about it. The group worker's emotional involvement, and tenuous control of the situation, felt dangerous but it was often salutary. Caseworkers who have moved into service with groups have experienced this sense of danger as the feeling, "there are so many of them and only one of me!"[62] They have found that

> . . . the group leadership role demands that the worker give up much of the interview control to which she has, often unconsciously, become accustomed. Caseworkers have often told me that they had never realized how rigidly they controlled the client-worker interaction until they began to function as group workers, where changes of subject could be effected by anyone in the group, where people often turned to each other rather than to the worker for reinforcement and support, where clients could verify each other's "wrong" ideas, where

> mutually reinforced feelings could not be turned off when they became "dangerous," and where, in short, one's faith in the client's autonomy and basic strength were put to its severest test.[63]

These are the themes of shared control, shared power, and the shared agenda, which are among those I have tried to identify in this paper. That their appearance is so disconcerting to those who first move into group service speaks well for their potential uses in helping to evolve a richer model of the helping process in social work. Each theme needs to be explored in some detail: the social self, the faith in action, the helping relationship as a reciprocal system, the shared power, the sense of immediacy, the eclecticism, the collective sources of individual strength, and even, in some respects, the didacticism that pervaded the group workers' outlook.

The ideas themselves are not new; many have in certain ways been accepted over the years. But they are easy to lose sight of, in a model of practice—perhaps it is the coveted medical model—of a unilateral power exercised over an objectified, inert, malleable client. For example, the definition of the self as a social creation, culturally formed and culturally modifiable, is well ensconced in today's scientific atmosphere; but it is hard to keep before us in the paradigm of the client as a broken object who comes to be repaired by an agent of change who operates single-handedly on self-contained, privately-owned personalities.

As to what it is that does help people change in their own chosen direction,[64] that question will be with us for a long time. The group workers' experience told them that there was something in the nature of *doing*, and particularly collective doing, that helped people find new ways of looking at themselves and the world around them. Many, like Neva Boyd, suspected verbal and logical explanations that went under the name of "insight," but seemed to produce more "aha"s than lasting changes in problem-solving behavior. And it was Kierkegaard, a generation before Freud, who said that "truth exists for the individual only as he himself produces it in action."[65] Ultimately, of course, the answer will lie not in pitting action against insight, but in finding the connections between the two, and the techniques with which to distinguish real understanding from verbal games, and meaningful action from a mechanical behaviorism.

And so it would go: there is obviously a great deal more to be done with these issues than can be attempted here. The major threads are reciprocal, systemic, existential, and would lead us back into studies that might rescue these constructs from their stereotypes and translate them back into their implications for practice, both one-to-one and one-to-group. For the present, this brief analysis may help bring their roots in the group work experience back into view and lead the profession forward in the process of locating the traditions that indeed make up the profession.

FOOTNOTES AND REFERENCES

1. Kathleen Woodroofe, *From Charity to Social Work* (Toronto: University of Toronto Press, 1962), p. 46.

2. Robert H. Bremner, *American Philanthropy* (Chicago: The University of Chicago Press, 1960), pp. 95 ff.

3. American Association of Social Workers, *Social Case Work, Generic and Specific: An Outline: A Report of the Milford Conference,* 1929, 92 pages.

4. "The TIAC Report: Principles, Proposals and Issues in Inter-Association Cooperation," *Social Work Journal*, Vol. 32, No. 3 (July 1951), pp. 112-57. Entire issue on the subject.

5. Melvin A. Glasser, "The Story of the Movement for a Single Professional Association," *Social Work Journal*, Vol. 36, No. 3 (July 1955), pp. 115-22.

6. Talcott Parsons, "A Sociologist Looks at the Legal Profession," in *Essays in Sociological Theory* (Glencoe, Ill.: The Free Press, 1954, Rev. Ed.), p. 372.

7. *See,* for example: Harriet M. Bartlett, "Toward Clarification and Improvement of Social Work Practice," *Social Work,* Vol. 3, No. 2 (April 1958), pp. 3-9. *See* also: her "The Generic-Specific Concept in Social Work Education and Practice," in Alfred J. Kahn (ed.), *Issues in American Social Work* (New York: Columbia University Press, 1959), pp. 159-90.

8. William E. Gordon, "A Critique of the Working Definition," *Social Work,* Vol. 7, No. 4 (October 1962), pp. 3-13.

9. For an earlier historical effort of my own, *see:* William Schwartz, "Group Work and the Social Scene," in Alfred E. Kahn (ed.), *Issues in American Social Work* (New York: Columbia University Press, 1959), pp. 110-37.

10. Henrietta Barnett, *Canon Barnett, His Life, Work, and Friends, By His Wife* (Boston and New York: Houghton Mifflin Company, 1919, 2 Volumes), Vol. I, pp. 27 ff.

11. Mary E. Richmond, *Social Diagnosis* (New York: Russell Sage Foundation, 1917).

12. Grace L. Coyle, *Social Process in Organized Groups* (New York: Richard R. Smith, 1930).

13. Henrietta Barnett, op. cit., p. 184.

14. *See*: Mrs. Glendower Evans, "Scientific Charity," *Proceedings of the National Conference of Charities and Correction, 1889* (Boston: Geo. H. Ellis, 1889), pp. 24-35.

15. *See*: William Schwartz, "Camping," *Social Work Year Book, 1960* (New York: National Association of Social Workers, 1960), pp. 112-17.

16. Margaretta Williamson, *The Social Worker in Group Work* (New York and London: Harper, 1929), p. 17.

17. William Heard Kilpatrick, *Group Education for a Democracy* (New York: Association Press, 1940), p. vii.

18. Grace Coyle, "On Becoming Professional," in *Toward Professional Standards* (New York: American Association of Group Workers, 1947), pp. 17-18.

19. Schwartz, "Group Work and the Social Scene," op. cit., p. 123.

20. For the distinction between the "priests," who minister to the needy without judging

them, and the "prophets," who thunder and hold up standards to follow, *see*: Clarke A. Chambers, "An Historical Perspective on Political Action *vs*. Individualized Treatment," in *Current Issues in Social Work Seen in Historical Perspective* (New York: Council on Social Work Education, 1962), p. 54.

21. Quoted in Clarke A. Chambers, *Seedtime of Reform: American Social Service and Social Action, 1918-1933* (Minneapolis: University of Minnesota Press, 1963), p. 150.

22. Ibid., p. 149.

23. Eduard C. Lindeman, "Group Work and Democracy—A Philosophical Note," reprinted in Albert S. Alissi (ed.), *Perspectives on Social Group Work Practice* (New York: The Free Press, 1980), p. 81. Originally published in 1939.

24. Jane Addams, *Twenty Years at Hull House* (New York: The New American Library, A Signet Classic, 1960), p. 97. First published in 1910.

25. Henrietta Barnett, *Canon Barnett, His Life, Work, and Friends. . . .*, op. cit., p. 110.

26. Henrietta Barnett, "Principles of Recreation," in Canon and Mrs. S. A. Barnett, *Towards Social Reform* (New York: The Macmillan Company, 1909), p. 289.

27. Eduard C. Lindeman, "Organization and Technique for Rural Recreation," *Proceedings of the National Conference of Social Work* (Chicago: University of Chicago Press, 1920), p. 321.

28. Henrietta Barnett, *Canon Barnett, His Life, Work, and Friends. . . .*, op. cit., p. 115.

29. Canon Barnett, "'Settlements' or 'Missions'," in Canon and Mrs. S. A. Barnett, op. cit., p. 273.

30. Ibid., pp. 271-88.

31. Charles Horton Cooley, *Social Organization: A Study of the Larger Mind* (New York: Schocken Books, 1962), p. 23. First published in 1909, by Charles Scribner's Sons.

32. Ibid., p. 29. Emphasis in original.

33. Ibid., p. 23.

34. James Mark Baldwin, *The Individual and Society* (Boston: Richard G. Badger, The Gorham Press, 1911), p. 16.

35. P. Kropotkin, *Mutual Aid, A Factor of Evolution* (New York: Alfred A. Knopf, 1925).

36. John Dewey, *Human Nature and Conduct* (New York: Random House, 1922).

37. George Herbert Mead, *Mind, Self and Society* (Chicago: University of Chicago Press, 1934).

38. Muzafer Sherif, *The Psychology of Social Norms* (New York: Harper, 1936).

39. Kurt Lewin, "Conduct, Knowledge, and Acceptance of New Values," in *Resolving Social Conflicts: Selected Papers on Group Dynamics* (New York: Harper, 1948), pp. 56-68.

40. Baldwin, op. cit., p. 16.

41. Mary Parker Follett, "Constructive Conflict," in Henry C. Metcalf and L. Urwick (eds.), *Dynamic Administration: The Collected Papers of Mary Parker Follett* (New York and London: Harper, 1940), p. 45. Paper first published in 1926.

42. Martin Buber, *I and Thou* (New York: Charles Scribner's Sons, 1958).

43. Neva L. Boyd, "The Social Education of Youth Through Recreation: The Value of Play in Education," in Paul Simon (ed.), *Play and Game Theory in Group Work: A Collection of Papers by Neva Leona Boyd* (Chicago: The Jane Addams Graduate School of Social Work at the University of Illinois at Chicago Circle, 1971), p. 43. Paper written in 1924.

44. Neva L. Boyd, "Social Group Work: A Definition With a Methodological Note," in Paul Simon (ed.), op. cit., p. 149. Paper written in 1937.

45. Ibid.

46. LeRoy E. Bowman, "Dictatorship, Democracy, and Group Work in America," *Proceedings of the National Conference of Social Work* (Chicago: University of Chicago Press, 1935), p. 385.

47. Virginia P. Robinson, "The Dynamics of Supervision under Functional Controls,"

in *The Development of a Professional Self: Teaching and Learning in Professional Helping Processes, Selected Writings, 1930-1968* (New York: AMS Press, 1978), p. 254. Article first published in 1948.

48. Grace Longwell Coyle, *Group Work With American Youth: A Guide to the Practice of Leadership* (New York: Harper, 1948), p. 32.

49. LeRoy Bowman, op. cit., p. 383.

50. For a discussion of this "symbiotic" relationship between the individual and his group, *see:* William Schwartz, "The Social Worker in the Group," *The Social Welfare Forum, 1961* (New York and London: Columbia University Press, 1961), pp. 156 ff.

51. For a discussion of the social work function in regard to the needs of the one and the many, *see:* William Schwartz, "Private Troubles and Public Issues: One Social Work Job or Two?" *The Social Welfare Forum, 1969* (New York and London: Columbia University Press, 1969), pp. 22-43.

52. Henrietta Barnett, *Canon Barnett, His Life, Work, and Friends. . .* .op. cit., p. 169.

53. Mrs. Glendower Evans, op. cit., p. 25.

54. Sigmund Freud, "The Dynamics of the Transference," (1912), *Collected Papers* (London: The Hogarth Press and The Institute of Psycho-Analysis, 1950, 5 Volumes), Vol. II, pp. 312-22.

55. Ibid., p. 318.

56. Sigmund Freud, "Recommendations for Physicians on the Psycho-Analytic Method of Treatment," (1912) *Collected Papers* (London: The Hogarth Press and The Institute of Psycho-Analysis, 1950, 5 Volumes), Vol. II, p. 331.

57. LeRoy Bowman, op. cit., pp. 385-6.

58. Mary Parker Follett, "Some Discrepancies in Leadership Theory and Practice," in Metcalf and Urwick (eds.), op. cit., p. 272. Emphasis in original. Article first published in 1928.

59. Grace Longwell Coyle, *Group Work With American Youth. . .* , op. cit., p. 216.

60. Frank J. Bruno (with chapters by Louis Towley), *Trends in Social Work, 1874-1956* (New York: Columbia University Press, 1957), p. 422.

61. Warren G. Bennis & H. A. Shepard, "A Theory of Group Development," *Human Relations,* Vol. 9 (1956), pp. 415-37.

62. William Schwartz, "Discussion of Three Papers on the Group Method with Clients, Foster Families, and Adoptive Families," *Child Welfare,* Vol. 45, No. 10 (December 1966), p. 572.

63. Ibid., p. 575.

64. *See,* for example: Allen Wheelis, "How People Change ," *Commentary* (May 1969), pp. 56-66.

65. Quoted in Rollo May, "The Emergence of Existential Psychology," in Rollo May, (ed.), *Existential Psychology* (New York: Random House, 1961), p. 12.

EIGHTH ANNUAL SYMPOSIUM ON THE ADVANCEMENT OF SOCIAL WORK WITH GROUPS

October 23-26, 1986
Los Angeles

A CALL FOR PRESENTATIONS

CREATIVE CONNECTIONS: ADVANCING THEORY AND PRACTICE

This symposium will provide a forum to enhance the integration of theory and practice in social work with groups.

Papers, workshops and panels will focus on the use of group process with a continuum of groups including: socialization, support, self-help, treatment, rehabilitation, teams and task groups in organizations and communities. Presentations should highlight concepts and interventions which are transferable within this continuum.

Abstracts should delineate and examine practice and theory in relation to generic concepts and practice with specific populations, cultures, types of groups or settings. We encourage submission of abstracts which reflect what current practice offers to support theory. Collaborative efforts are welcome. Presentations are encouraged which highlight group work with vulnerable populations including age groups, ethnic populations, refugees, the disabled and other at-risk groups. Papers and presentations dealing with innovations in work with groups in the fields of Health, Education/Socialization, Mental Health, Work with Families and Children, Community Work, and Industrial settings are sought.

Abstracts should be five hundred words long and discuss the main topic and basic premises. The major concepts, types of intervention, types of groups or special populations should be described. Please indicate practice issues, theory base, and where applicable, research base. In addition a fifty word summary of the abstract must accompany each submission.

Abstracts are to be submitted no later than February 15, 1986. Notification of acceptance will be made by April 15, 1986. Three copies of completed papers (approximate length 15 pages) or details of other types of presentations are due on June 30th, 1986. Acceptance of the abstract guarantees a place on the final program, providing the completed paper or details of other types of presentations is consistent with the approved abstract.

Send abstract and papers to: Dr. Marie Weil, School of Social Work, Montgomery Ross Fisher Building, University of Southern California, University Park, Los Angeles 90089-0411.

For further information contact: Dr. Helen Northen or Marie Weil, Conference Co-Chairpersons, or Dr. Florence Clemenger, Chairperson Program Committee at the same address, telephone (213) 743-2711.

The Eighth Annual Symposium is sponsored jointly by the following organizations: The Committee for the Advancement of Social Work With Groups, The Journal of Social Work with Groups, The Haworth Press, and The School of Social Work of the University of Southern California in cooperation with the Schools of Social Work at the University of California, Los Angeles; The University of Utah; University of California, Berkeley; California State University at Long Beach, Fresno and Sacramento; The University of Hawaii; The University of Denver; Portland State University; and The University of Washington.

The Reciprocal Model: A Change in the Paradigm

Alex Gitterman

Social group work emerged from the settlement, Y's and community centers, also recreation and progressive education movements. From the settlements, group work derived its institutional base. Its leadership was committed to the development of responsible citizenship, assimilation, participation in democratic processes, and collective action. Participation in democratic, mutual aid group processes was the primary mechanism for achieving these valued outcomes.[1] From the recreation movement, social group work developed its interest in the value of play, leisure-time activities, body movement and physical action. Camping emphasized the child's transaction with the natural world, its appreciation and effective uses. Recreational needs and outlets were used to "build character" and develop a sense of competence and mastery.[2] From progressive education, social group work acquired a philosophical base emphasizing the uses of mutual aid and peer learning. To participate and experience democratic discussions and learning was considered to be the most effective method for preparing America's youth to function in a democratic society.[3]

For several decades, practitioners and educators from settlements, Y's, recreation, camping and education struggled to develop an integrating theoretical foundation for diverse practice contexts. Using knowledge and research findings primarily from sociology, social psychology, and education, a social group work literature emerged. Some defined group work as a field of practice; others as a social movement in the pursuit of democratic living and social reform; and, still others identified group work as a distinct process and method. To incorporate these diverse (but also congruent) traditions, group work's boundaries and functions were defined by broad premises and goals. These were in the foreground; professional methodology remained in the background and less attended.

In the early '60's, the writings of Schwartz and Vinter received

© 1986 by The Haworth Press, Inc. All rights reserved.

wide attention and interest because of their common concerns and commitment to the development of a professional methodology. Vinter moved toward re-specifying the more established casework "psycho-social" paradigm of social study, diagnosis and treatment.[4] Schwartz proposed a bold and ambitious paradigm which provoked excitement and debate and endures as a strong influence upon practice.[5] The purpose of this paper is to elucidate Schwartz' central ideas and their significance for practice.

Social Work Function

In describing her mission at Hull House, Jane Addams wrote:

> Hull House endeavors to make social intercourse express the growing sense of the economic unity of society . . . It was opened on the theory that dependence of classes on each other is reciprocal.[6]

Schwartz wove this vision and notion of reciprocity into the fabric of his writing. He proposed the idea of a "symbiotic" relationship between individual and societal needs.

> This presupposes a relationship between the individual and his nurturing group that can be described as symbiotic . . . each needs the other for its own life and growth and each reaches out to the other with all possible strength at a given moment.[7]

Using systems theory, Schwartz suggested the individual possesses a natural impetus "toward health, growth and belonging," and a similar natural impetus of society to "integrate its parts into a productive and dynamic whole."[8] In a complex society, this reciprocal relationship may become tenuous, diffuse and obscure. And Schwartz asserted that the obstacles to reciprocal individual/societal need fulfillment provide social work with a distinctive professional function: to mediate the transactions between individual member needs and group requirements; and between group needs and agency services. Essentially, Schwartz assigns the profession the function of mediating between these diverse and competing interests and demands.

This straightforward conception of professional function leads to other powerful ideas. In carrying out this conception of professional function, the worker, for example, though representing the employing organization, avoids the "mistake" of identifying with either the organization or the client. He identifies with the need for them to engage each other. For if workers align themselves with clients and "disown" their agencies, they attenuate their credibility and effectiveness in helping clients use the resources of the agency. If workers align themselves with the organization and "become" the organization, they lose their ability to engage clients. The professional task, therefore, is to represent the organization without becoming or disowning it. By assigning the profession a "mediating" function, Schwartz offers a viable and heuristic although quite complex, functional statement:

> The practitioner is required neither to change the system nor to change the people but to change the ways in which they deal with each other.[9]

This conception differentiates social work from other professions and offers a distinctive function in the division of labor among professions. The emphasis upon changing maladaptive ways in which individuals and systems deal with each other rather than on the pathology of either provides for the profession to be equally concerned with prevention as well as rehabilitation, with normal developmental concerns as well as pathology and with "private troubles" as well as "public issues."

Mutual Aid

The formed and natural group serves as the primary medium for the individual/social exchange. People experiencing others in the "same boat" in the "rocky waters" of life, struggling with similar issues and concerns, have the opportunity to evolve a mutual aid system. Schwartz envisages this potential in any group.

> Ideally, any group can establish reciprocal helping relationships among its members and become a system of mutual aid wherein members extend help to each other in working out their common problems.[10]

As people confide, share and move into taboo areas, they perceive themselves not being alone, their concerns not being unique and their problems not being necessarily pathological. By its very nature, the mutual aid group system universalizes people's troubles and reduces isolation and stigma. These processes release the group's potential for a multiplicity of helping relationships. The worker is not the only one assigned the responsibility for helping; every member is also assigned this task.

> The important fact is that this is a helping system in which clients need each other as well as the worker. This need to use each other, to create not one but many helping relationships is a vital ingredient of the group process and constitutes a common need over and above the specific tasks for which the group was formed.[11]

As members become invested in and committed to the mutual aid system, they are compelled to examine their perceptions and behaviors and to rehearse and experiment with more adaptive responses.

As people develop comfort in being together and a greater openness to examine their perceptions and behaviors, they simultaneously develop a sense of collective strength and power. Usually, the strength of this mutual bond and alliance is tested against the worker's authority. When successfully accomplished, the "taking and sharing" of power propels group members to a more intimate and personal level. This process simultaneously provides members more confidence to actively deal with and gain mastery over environmental obstacles. Since collective action has greater visibility (and mitigates individual isolation and possible reprisals from authority), the group becomes a powerful force for organizational and social influence and change.

Method

Schwartz conceptualized a social work method and not just a group work method. He was committed to developing a common language for social workers in which practitioners would be able to talk to each other about what they do and build on each other's experience and skills. In engaging the tasks of specifying the worker's "actions" and the technical problems of developing a professional method, he emphasized the use of *verbs* to transform professional knowledge, sensitivity, goals and philosophy, into specific and particular actions in the helping process.

> There are "knowers" who cannot help anybody and there are "feelers" who cannot put their feelings to use in the service of people . . . The client is not interested in his worker's store of knowledge, in his aspirations for humanity, or even in his degree of self-awareness; always his questions will be: does he seem to know what to do for me, and has he been able to help me?[12]

In the helping process, helping and using help are interdependent and differentiated. They are conceptualized as a parallel process with worker and client each assuming separate tasks and behaviors: a worker struggling to help; a client deciding whether to use or not to use the help at a given time and from a particular person. Thus, the professional actions may be skillful and the client may regress; they may be unskillful and the client may progress. To develop an objective, accountable, transferable and, most of all, a teachable professional method, our behaviors have to be conceptualized and evaluated in their own terms and analytically distinguished from intent or actual outcomes.

Contract: A Phase in the Helping Process

Schwartz classified the helping process into four interrelated and distinct phases: the preparatory "tuning-in" phase through which the worker prepares him/herself to move into the group experience; the "contract" phase through which group members, worker and agency make their beginnings; the "work" phase in which group purpose is operationalized; and finally, the "termination" phase in which members separate and the group ends (or the worker leaves).[13] In this presentation, only the second phase, contract (a distinctive contribution of Schwartz) will be examined. The idea has had a powerful and lasting impact upon practice.

In the second phase, the worker attempts to help members develop a clear focus and identify the conditions of their work. Through a contracting process, the purpose and roles of agency, worker and members converge and are specified. Essentially, contract refers to a clear-cut and mutually developed consensus about group purpose and focus.

> The contract, openly reflecting both stakes, provides the frame of reference for the work that follows, and for understanding

> when the work is in process, when it is being evaded, and when it is finished.[14]

A simple, straightforward statement connects the group members' *needs*, the agency's *assignment* and the social worker's *function*. Schwartz suggested four specific contracting steps: (1) to make a clear statement of why the service was being offered; (2) to describe the worker's role in the agency and group; (3) to encourage reaction to the statement and how it fits in with their own understanding and wishes; and (4) to come to agreement on the terms and the frame of reference for working together.[15]

To illustrate: a group service was offered to sixth grade youngsters experiencing difficulty in an urban junior high school:

> Charles said, "You mean we're not going to play basketball?" I answered, "This group will not be like a community center club, because the community center is there for that." I continued, "The school wants you to have a chance to talk about some of the things that are bothering you about school." Their facial expressions spoke loudly. Bill and George and some of the others wanted this kind of chance to talk about school problems. Charles and a couple of the others wanted fun doing recreational type of things. I asked, "You're afraid that talking about what is on your minds about school won't be fun?" They acknowledged that they didn't think it would be fun. I said that we had hoped that this kind of thing would make school more fun for them. This sounded possible to them and George said, "Well, what will we do?" I replied, "Let's see if I can explain. We can get together and talk about the troubles you're having in school, and things that are on your minds, and while we do it, we might find reasons for some of those problems." Bill asked, "Do you mean we tell you our problems and you tell us what to do about them?" I answered that that wasn't it, but he was close. I said, "I'm here to help you say what you're thinking, to help you think about what you can do. You have to do the thinking 'cause you know what the problems are like." Bill said, "Oh, I get it. This will help us pass school." I said, "I hope so. Sounds like you're all afraid that you won't pass the sixth grade." Remarks came fast. "Boy, are we!" "We're lucky to get this far." I said, "It's a scary thing to think about failing." Charles said, "Yeah, my folks. . . " Charles and John both made statements that their folks would kill them if

> they didn't pass. I said, "This would be one of the reasons for the club—to help you pass." After a long silence, Eddie said, "You can make us pass?" in a hopeful tone. I said, "Wait a minute, I can't do miracles. I can't change you into A students—you have problems getting in your way. They're your problems and only you can try to solve them. You can give each other ideas, and I can give you some, too, but you have to do the work on trying them out." There were comments that sounded like: "Let's give it a try." "Sounds good."
>
> I asked if they wanted to see what if would be like. They all anxiously said they would. I asked if anyone right now could think of anything that was bothering him in school. They all thought it was too difficult for them. I asked if they wanted me to give an example. All said, "Yes." "Okay," I said, "Suppose I was in your school and had something on my mind. Maybe I had a fight with my brother. Even if I wanted to think about my studies, I can't because I can't stop thinking about how I would like to get even with my brother." Bill broke in and said, "You can't do the writing." I continued, "Okay, I can't think about the writing. And the teacher comes along and I get into trouble. I get mad because she doesn't understand that I have something that bothers me." Every ear was involved, and it seemed real to them. Their remarks came fast. "Those teachers are mean sometimes." "Yeah, that Mr. Johnson, he's mean."[16]

The agency offer of service and members' perception of needs do not represent a contract until a mutual agreement has been reached about their foci and methods. For the understanding to have meaning, it has to be specific and clear. By offering a specific example, prepared in the tuning-in phase, the worker helps group members experience what they had been trying to define and understand. The clear focus provides the youngsters with a common frame of reference and a structure for their discussion, thereby decreasing anxiety associated with fear of a "hidden agenda" or the unknown and the ambiguity inherent in all beginnings.

Conclusion

In developing his ideas, Schwartz moved away from the more comfortable and well established paradigms. Understandably, his ideas were criticized by those identified with some of the more established social casework traditions as well as the less well established social action community organization tradition. The former criticized him for an inadequate attention to assessment of individual behavior; the latter criticized him for a limited attention to the political social change agenda. While these concerns had validity, they tended to be generalized and dismissive, failing to recognize his imaginative and useful effort to put forth a distinctive social work function which attempted to integrate rather than dichotomize the individual/social relationship.

Schwartz' closest and most appreciative academic colleagues, however, were uneasy about his extending the idea of symbiosis in a small face to face group to describe the relationship between individuals and their social institutions and the broader social context. Schwartz argued that the symbiotic relationship did exist: children, for example, needed the school to learn; the school needed children to teach. This relationship reflected, however, what should be or "ought" to be rather than capture the reality, the "is", in which the children have significantly less resources and power than their teachers. Often a clear conflict of interest exists. Parasitic relationships are as likely as symbiotic ones. The strength in Schwartz' argument, however, was that the symbiotic potential provided the worker with a vision of a reciprocal relationship, and, therefore, a clear and viable professional function.

In his writing, teaching and professional discourse, Schwartz charted new directions, broke theoretical ground and made a profound contribution to professional practice and education. His writing was eloquent in its clarity, simplicity and vitality. This article attempts to capture some of his powerful and lasting ideas about social work.

NOTES

1. See, for example, Jane Addams, *Twenty Years at Hull House,* New York: MacMillan, 1910; Jane Addams, *The Second Twenty Years at Hull House,* New York: MacMillan, 1930; Arthur Holder, *The Settlement Idea—A Vision of Social Justice,* New York: MacMillan, 1915; Lillian Wald, *The House on Henry Street,* New York: Holt, 1915.

2. See, for example, Joseph Lee, *Play in Education,* New York: MacMillan, 1915; Joshua Lieberman, *Creative Camping,* New York: Association Press, 1931.

3. See, for example, John Dewey, *Democracy and Education,* New York: MacMillan, 1916; Mary Follet, *Creative Experience,* New York: Longmans, Green, 1924; Robert MacIver, *Community,* New York: MacMillan, 1924; Edward Lindeman, *Social Discovery,* New York: Republic, 1924.

4. Robert Vinter, "Group Work Perspectives and Prospects," *Social Work with Groups 1959,* New York: N.A.S.W., 1959; "Social Group Work," *Encylopedia of Social Work,* New York: N.A.S.W., 1965, 715-24.

5. For elaboration of historical discussion, see, Alex Gitterman, "Group Work Content in an Integrated Method Curriculum," *Social Work with Groups, Proceedings, 1979 Symposium,* eds. Sonia Abels and Paul Abels. Louisville, Kentucky: Committee for Advancement of Social Work with Groups, 1979, pp. 66-81.

6. Jane Addams, *A Centennial Reader.* New York: MacMillan, 1960, p. 10

7. William Schwartz, "Social Group Work: Interactionist Approaches," *Social Work Encyclopedia.* New York: N.A.S.W., 1971, p. 1259.

8. William Schwartz, "The Social Worker in the Group," *The Social Welfare Forum, 1961.* New York: Columbia University Press, 1961, p. 9.

9. William Schwartz, "Private Troubles and Public Issues: *One Social Work Job or Two?" Social Welfare Forum,* 1969, p. 41.

10. William Schwartz, "The Social Worker in the Group," *New Perspectives on Services to Groups.* New York: National Association of Social Workers, 1961, p. 13.

11. William Schwartz, *ibid.,* p. 12.

12. William Schwartz, "The Classroom Teaching of Social Work with Groups: Some Central Problems," unpublished paper presented at Council on Social Work Education Faculty Day, Toronto, Canada, January 1964, p. 4.

13. William Schwartz, "On the Use of Groups in Social Work Practice," *The Practice of Group Work,* William Schwartz and Serapio Zalba, ed.s. New York: Columbia University Press, 1971, pp. 13-18.

14. *Ibid.,* p. 8

15. *Ibid.,* p. 15

16. Alex Gitterman, "Group Work in the Public Schools," *ibid.,* pp. 54-56.

Call for Papers

Social Work with Groups announces a forthcoming special issue for which papers will now be accepted for Volume 11, No. 1, Spring 1988.

GROUP WORK PRACTICE FOR THE PREVENTION OF VIOLENCE AND TREATMENT OF VICTIMS

Guest Editor: Professor George S. Getzel, D.S.W.
Hunter College
School of Social Work
129 East 79 Street
New York, New York 10021

Possible topics include group work practice with the following:

— Child Abuse
— Spousal abuse
— Crime against the elderly
— Rape victims
— Homicide survivors
— Elder abuse
— Children in war zones
— Victims of street crime
— Violence against gays and lesbians
— Violence against the disabled

DEADLINE: January 30, 1987.

Seeing It Whole: Social Work with Groups Within an Integrative Perspective

Judith A.B. Lee

Special leaders with the unique talent of "seeing it whole" have risen amongst us at critical points in the history and development of the social work profession. In 1942, Bertha Reynolds shared her vision that "the whole was more than the sum of its parts." Her recognition that "group relations are inseparable from individual ones" and that social group work "is ahead (of social casework) in the appreciation and use of knowledge of mores and cultures and is at least as far advanced in the practice of democracy in human relationships" led her to see social group work and community organization as "the growing edge" of social work. It also led her to entitle her 1942 landmark work *Learning And Teaching in the Practice of Social Work* when there was yet no unified concept of social work practice as greater than the sum of its separate "primary methods" parts, social casework, social groupwork and community organization. It was her belief, in view of the context of her times, that ". . . It is important that the whole of social work move forward, emphasizing common elements rather than differences" (Reynolds, 1942, p.11).

The generic vision, born with different yet related meaning at the Milford conference of 1929 was embraced and elaborated by far-sighted leaders like Reynolds and others. For example, in 1955 Trecker and other social group work leaders saw a frontier for social group work as "stepping up the identification of group workers with social work as a whole. Many suggested that we should spell out the contribution that we may make as group workers to generic social work" (Trecker, 1955, p.383).

But it was William Schwartz who made the greatest contribution to the generic vision as we know it today for he not only "lent us his vision," he defined social work function and operationalized the

© 1986 by The Haworth Press, Inc. All rights reserved.

tasks of the social worker in carrying out that function. In 1959 while other group worker's were still defining "social group work" method he noted that "there are those who are convinced that the helping process itself is essentially generic and that the time is not far off when a social work method can be developed and taught" (Schwartz, 1959, p. 137). Further he emphasized the unique contribution which group work gave to the profession of social work. "It served to expand the scope of social work itself, bringing it back to earlier and broader conceptions of its function and responsibility at a time when these were being interpreted in ever narrowing terms. It brought fresh sociological thinking into a profession that was coming more and more to explain human behavior and social phenomena in biological and individualistic terms, it carried a renewed interest in social treatment, where the emphasis had been shifting almost entirely to individual therapy . . ." (Schwartz, 1959, p. 123-124). How pertinent to the current scene! How important it is to reaffirm the special contributions of groupwork to the vision of generic social work. And, how important it is not to lose the generic vision while affirming our contribution to it.

For Schwartz noted as early as 1961 that the moment had passed for defining the social group work method. He argued, with his typical foresight, that the time had come for defining that which is generic to all social work helping, regardless of the number of people in the relational system at hand (Schwartz, 1961, p. 211). Further, he ventured a statement of professional function which pulled together the diverse threads of social work thinking into a new unity which no longer split the individual and the social but found the link between them, and placed the social worker at that point of intervention. "We would suggest that the general assignment for the social work profession is to mediate the process through which the individual and his society reach out for each other through a mutual need for self-fulfillment. The social worker's intervention lies at the point where two forces meet: the individuals' impetus toward health, growth and belonging, and the organized efforts of society to integrate its parts into a productive and dynamic whole" (Schwartz, 1961, p. 215). His delineation of the professional tasks which follow from this function (Schwartz, 1961, p. 217) remove his approach from mere abstraction and enables us to conceptualize our actual doing in order to realize our professional assignment. Later related theoretical formulations, such as the Life Model Approach of Carel Germain and Alex Gitterman, build, in part, on this basic formulation and elaborate it more fully. Together his thinking and theirs form a powerful statement of social work practice for our current times. This paper seeks to affirm Schwartz's vision of social work practice, his unique formulation in "seeing it whole", as well as his sense of the special contribution group work has made to the profession of social work.

For our leaders were indeed right and the time has come—we have "gone generic" which for some is the fulfillment (albeit imperfectly) of a dream; and for some more equivalent to the phrase "gone to the dogs". Many major schools of social work are teaching generic "Practice" courses in the first year or throughout the two years of the MSW curriculum. Yet with this realization of a vision has come the inevitable emergence of the dialectical process. Just as the need for a common method emerged when there were three "methods" (or five, depending on definition—see Smalley, 1969) and the need for a common core of knowledge and skill emerged when there were distinct fields of practice, so the opposite emerges now. Emanuel Tropp is asking, "What Ever Happened To Social Group Work?" and noting that it refused "to disappear under the generic blanket that began its banishment in the late 1960's" (Tropp, 1978). The Council on Social Work Education Curriculum Policy Statement of 1981 is moving back to "field of practice specialization" (CSWE, 1981). While this author accepts the inevitability of such dialectical forces which, in fact, move us slowly forward in theory building in a strange cyclical repetitive manner, she questions whether this plea to return to "the way it was" is, in fact, regressive and overly simplistic given the long worked for and definite establishment of the generic, or holistic, or integrative approaches to social work education and practice. One can have one's pick of the words preferred to describe the current state of the field for what each connotes somewhat differently is the ability of the social work profession to "see it whole." While a return to various notions of specialization represents seduction to return to times that offered a simplification of human and societal complexity and a dichotomizing of the professional function to mediate at the points of inseparable connection of these two (Schwartz, 1961, 1971).

In part, this regression occurs because seeing it whole makes terrific demands on the social work educator and practitioner. It demands that we teach and learn at a staggering level of complexity and ambiguity; that we need to know more than ever before; that we conceptualize at both the level of abstraction encompassing the clients whole field of being and at the level of particular interventions; and that we conceptualize the nature of the transactional arena of being instead of static and linear explanations of behavior and how to intervene. Related to the particular tensions of social work with groups and social work practice in general it demands, for example, that group dynamics and processes become a strong part of the Human Behavior foundation curriculum. How can one teach personality development without looking at it from the group dynamics and process point of view if the nature of social development is to be understood? Hartford cautioned, "I am afraid that we are reducing the content about small group process by default as we increase theory about individuals, families, social systems, and organizations—and have left small group theory as an elective." Further she has great concern that "we are lessening the amount of knowledge we are teaching about small groups . . . just at the moment when we are expecting all social workers to use more group methods . . ." (Hartford, 1978). In an unpublished study Karp (1979) found that working with groups was highly deemphasized in actual teaching in the generic curriculum which was taught mainly by people with casework background. Most group work educators have moved into positions of administration in the educational system. So, there is a fear, with some reality base, among those of us who value and are trained in social work with groups that "generic" or "integrative" means complete depletion.

Hence, some of us prefer a "micro" conceptualization, a two methods approach which preserves social casework and social group work as distinct (Tropp, 1978). This author would prefer instead that educators be given help in learning the method they may not be as familiar with in order to teach holistically in an integrative curriculum. Faculty Development is a necessary given in such situations. For as Middleman said, "I am less concerned with the survival of the social group method per se as a distinct specialization within social work than with the abandonment of its historic concern for the common developmental struggles of living through participant involvement in a group process." Group work is for *all* social workers to use according to what needs to be done rather than what they feel comfortable doing" (1978, p. 16).

It is indeed important to own our history and social group work's unique contribution to the field. It is beyond the scope of this paper to touch all the bases, but a few golden threads run clear through. From groupwork's inception with the English Friendly Societies and the Settlement House Movement here and abroad to the present time group work has provided human connection, relationship and mutual aid to all kinds of people struggling with the common tasks of living in "the demoralizing hugeness of industrial society" (Woodroofe, 1966, p. 73) currently characterized by "increasing anomie and alienation" (Papell and Rothman, 1978). Unique to the Settlement House Movement are the contributions of: (1) working with the competent as well as those in need; (2) the translation of democratic values into social work practice and (3) the use of many helping relationships, mutual aid. Much of this was in the context of social reform purposes. It was the first contribution, however, that made some group workers uneasy about identifying with social work. At the National Conference of Social Work in 1935 LeRoy Bowman urged that it was a mistake to identify group work with social services since "Groupwork is not primarily a service to those who ask for help—it is the social mechanism perfectly competent people utilize to achieve their own ends" (Alissi, p. 19). Indeed since the alliance with social work, group work did have to sink or swim in the psychiatric deluge described by Woodroofe (1966) and, like casework, experienced a pull and at times a loss of identity in the direction of a disease model which describes our help as treatment and our clients as patients even in settings like community centers and settlement houses! (Tropp, 1969). LeRoy Bowman was not that far off on the dangers of joining. But, he could not then have forecasted that social work could move forward as a whole to a conceptualization of practice that relates to normal human struggles with problems in living with a value on mutual aid and social networks, and beyond the disease model to an approach to social work practice that includes all fields of practice and all methods so that the workers could offer Middleman's "what needs to be done."

For example, the Life Model Approach to social work practice offers those of us who value group methods an anchoring in an integrative social work approach congruent with and in part built upon our own deepest historical roots and values (Germain and Gitterman, 1980). It is a positive destigmatized non-disease oriented view of people and of helping based on an ecological perspective—or seeing people and environments in some sort of adaptive fit. Germain, a caseworker and educator and Gitterman, a group worker and educator have in uniting provided us with a theoretical framework which conceptualizes human struggles in three interelated areas: the life transitional and developmental, the interpersonal, and the environmental. The social worker needs knowledge and skills to help clients in each area. Group services are useful and needed in each area, as well as direct work with individuals and families and in influencing larger institutions including one's own agency to better fit people. In their text Germain and Gitterman (1980) give a knowledge and skills base consistent with Schwartz's interactionist point of view (1971) with ample illustrative examples of groups at work. Reciprocity, mutuality, contracting and mediation are key concepts of the approach which can also be attributed directly to the influence of Schwartz's interactionist approach to social work with groups (1971). This is a social work model with a distinct group work heritage. The model's other key concepts—promoting competence, mastery, autonomy, identity, and human relatedness are also compatible with group work's history and value base.

I have written elsewhere on the helpfulness of the mutual aid group in promoting these ego strengths and in negotiating, or changing non-nutritive environments (see for example, Lee and Swenson, 1979). I think one example from practice will make the issues more real for us. In an article which first appeared in the *American Journal of Orthopsychiatry,* July 1978, entitled "A Group Approach To The Depressed Adolescent Girl in Foster Care," Park and I applied interactionist and life model concepts to our work with groups of older adolescent foster children. We found that there was a cyclical relationship between the support and help gained from the group in developing competence and identity and in the relief of depression related to the current situation and past losses. As depression was dealt with, coping abilities were freed. As coping is more effective, depression is further dispelled. Yet the most important feature of being in this group for the girls was the chance to re-form a nutritive family-like primary group structure. This helped restore and revitalize the members capacities for good human relatedness. Two examples of actual group process from that group will illustrate how such a group may work and the possible gains. The first example of mutual aid is from a middle phase group meeting, one girl is sharing a problem in fighting:

> Leticia explained, some fights are caused by someone making a remark about my mother. The kid would be joking and not know that I'm in foster care. I said, it must hurt and no one really knows why you are fighting. She went on about how she's always having to fight. Carin then asked, in exasperation, what's all this fighting about? I said, I wonder what

> Leticia is trying to tell us, perhaps we can figure it out together. It sounds like maybe Leticia feels she has to prove something. Carin said, you're just trying to prove that you're as good as them. Leticia was silent. Carin said, don't you know you're as good as anybody else—don't you know who you are? I said, this is part of what we're here for, to help figure out who we are. Maybe Leticia is fighting 'cause she doesn't like who she is—a foster kid. She replied, it makes me feel small. Carin suggested that she just walk away. I said, the feelings are rough and it isn't that easy for everyone. Silence. Millie then quietly said, being foster is like being a piece of garbage. You're just something somebody tossed out.

In this example we see the dual emphasis on coping more effectively and dealing with the painful identity issues of the foster child. Leticia is helped by the group to better negotiate her peer system. They share the pain of abandonment together which brings some healing. One could also envision the worker intervening in Leticia's world, mediating at school where her fighting interferes with her learning and that of her peers and where the classroom environment may or may not be a nutritive one; in the foster family where she may distance herself from caring or find difficulty in getting in; and with her natural family who represents the hoped for reunion along with frequent disappointment. An integrative approach provides for mediation on many levels. The distinctions between casework, groupwork, family work, systems work and community work are less important than the provision of a whole service to a whole human being. While some clients may be able to grow primarily from the group service, others may need a combination of approaches. One problem, however, in that particular agency, and it is not an unusual problem, was that the group service itself was seen as adjunctive. Workers were expected to provide many services but not the group service, it was seen as an "extra". This is ironic when we realize how unique the power of the primary group in working on painful issues and ultimately in restoring human connection and relatedness.

In their last meeting the girls shared their views on what the group meant to them:

> The mood was quiet, thoughtful, and very close. Leticia said with pride and determination, this group helped me to be different. I'm the only one in my family not pregnant, and I'm the

> only one going to college. Kenya said, yeah, me too. I never thought I'd even make it out of high school. I guess I never cared either. I used to run around and mess with dope and everything. But I did those things when I had nothing better to do, now I'm gonna give college a try. Carin said softly, life matters more now, not always, but more. When I become a doctor I'm gonna help a lot of people. Kenya said, I'll be your first patient—and everyone laughed. Millie, who steadily plugged away at school, said, no one at home thinks I can make it but I know now that I don't have to show them. Millie is going to make it for Millie! Glenda said, right on! and added, I love college and I think I may even become a social worker. Life is great, my foster mother loves and trusts me now more than ever! Her only complaint was that her younger sisters were in trouble and driving the family crazy. The agency ought to start a group for eleven and twelve year olds! Everyone agreed with her suggestion, saying they could have used it too. Cherise spoke of nursing school and of moving South with her foster family. Then she added quietly, I wish I could stay here with the group. I've changed in the group. I've grown from hate into kindness . . .

This very special growth "into kindness" or in the ability to love and feel loved is perhaps the most important gain of group membership. Clearly these youngsters were able to help each other grow. Yet I am struck with the fact that many agencies who have traditionally "done casework" and many instructors who are comfortable with only one modality would by design or default deny the group service to clients. But only offering a group service can also be a disservice. When an agency or educational institution is wedded to any process or method ideology there is a real danger that client needs are secondary to the needs of workers and educators to practice and teach their modalities. I see the group as a primary vehicle for service, or in medical language, as a "treatment of choice" for many if not most clients. I am also well aware of the struggle in agencies and in academia to *equally* value and prepare practitioners for group work. Groupwork most often gets the "short end of the stick." Yet, I feel there must be a word of caution around specialization. Case after case, or group after group if you will, can be cited which demonstrated well the unique offering of the group to its members. From a practice base as well as a theoretical base it can be demonstrated that group modality must have equal value and space in an integrative curriculum and in the repertoire of the social work practitioner. But, our clients are fragmented enough, the social work practitioner, therefore, needs fluency in the various ways of serving clients to do "what needs to be done". Integrative approaches such as the interactionist and life model approach give us a framework from which to proceed.

The arenas for practice in this approach are congruent with places group workers have always been-in the actual life spaces of the client. For children, for example, that would mean to be in the play area, the friendship group, the neighborhood, the community center, the school and the family (Lee, 1981). The use of natural groups and formed groups at points of transition in the client's life is valued. For adults, social work services can be in the home, in the work place, in the neighborhood, in the place of worship or recreation as well as in the agency. Weiner's location of the social work role in industrial social welfare, in unions and actual work place is the kind of thinking this model employs. There is an emphasis on finding and building upon natural helping networks (Swenson, 1979).

In such an approach the skills of working with natural groups and of promoting mutual aid in both natural and formed groups is valued. The service may be located at points of prevention such as with "at risk teenage mothers"; or after serious problems in living have occurred such as with abusive parents or hospitalized mental patients; or at points where trouble may be expectable such as with recent retirees or stroke victims. It may have an environmental social action focus such as a tenants group or a group of concerned parents or a more individual transitional focus such as young adults having trouble leaving home. It may be at points of crisis, when sudden hazardous events strike (such as recently diagnosed cancer patients or rape victims), or at points of coping with ongoing struggle due to a status change such as becoming newly married or newly divorced or a foster child. The points of intervention are located throughout the life cycle both before, during and after trouble arises. It may have a social action, socialization or more insight oriented and support focus. It is a broad model reaching people where they live and offering mutual aid. It does not dichotomize person and situation but aims at relieving stress in both areas often simultaneously. All of our group work knowledge and skill can be utilized for the worker of this model is expected to have real facility with groups as well as individuals, families and systems (Germain and Gitterman, 1980, p. 29). The purpose is to mediate the connection between people and their systems in order to attain a better "goodness of fit." The point of intervention is always in the interactional area between the two. For this author, Shulman's work on elaborating skills of the interactionist approach (1979) (essentially again building on Schwartz's work) supply much of the skill for this approach. These are also elaborated within the life model approach itself (Germain and Gitterman, 1980). However, more knowledge of the transactional area and the nature of interventions in that area is also needed according to Germain and Gitterman. Perhaps those of us who tend to 'see it whole' and view the world systematically as group workers will be in a position to build knowledge in that transactional area. The person coming from this holistic perspective may also need to ground herself more in knowledge and skill related to the individual system as well since equal facility is expected.

The interactionist and life model approaches are seen as congruent with group work heritage, knowledge, skills and values, and are offered for investigation and to confirm our place within an integrative perspective to social work practice. With the concept of such a generic practice approach now conceptualized, today's students have it easier in some respects. But they also have a great deal more to learn and the burden on the teacher is great. The challenge is to teach in the particular while "seeing it whole." Generic or integrative practice can be learned, taught, and practiced without the sacrifice of group work's unique contribution and without the sacrifice of depth. In fact, one needs much depth to support a broad based model. If group work continues to own its heritage and to join with current overall social work approaches both will be more likely to survive in this current era so dangerous to social work's survival not to speak of human survival itself.

Whenever there is a union of separate entities, whether it be in marriage or other intimate joining of lives, or in family life or in small or large groups, there is a tension. A pull between the healthy movement toward individual autonomy and the equally normal desire to be part of a group, to join with the other, to establish the system that is more than the sum of its parts. The union of social group work with social work has meant some loss of identity since groupwork had not quite consolidated its own identity before joining. Group work, therefore, needs to continue to identify its distinct contributions and hold on to its uniqueness more than it has.

Schwartz's interactionist approach, the contribution of Papell and Rothman in synthesizing and integrating our "Mainstream Model" (Papell and Rothman, 1980) and the work of Norma Lang on "A Broad-Range Model" (1974) and her continued work on theory building are landmark steps in that direction. This author's only caution is that group work theory be 'plugged into' an overall integrative perspective of social work practice. For there is more to the client's world than group affiliation, however central this is. Papell and Rothman noted the explosion of knowledge in the 1970's, while Germain noted the explosion of ignorance as well which led to a proliferation of "models" and an emphasis on theoretical differences rather than similarities. While Papell and Rothman state that by now it is hard to simplify all of our knowledge into two or three approaches, in this author's view they are also correct in assessing that "there is a need now to establish anew the essential identity of social work practice with groups even as the process of differentiating within the whole continues" (1980, p. 6). That is, we must continue to be part of a holistic social work approach, (the interactionist and life model approaches are offered as particularly congruent for group workers) while maintaining the uniqueness of group work's contribution to any overall approach to social work practice.

REFERENCES

Allissi, A.S. *Perspectives on Social Group Work Practice.* New York: The Free Press, 1980.

Germain C. & Gitterman, A. *The Life Model of Social Work Practice.* New York: Columbia University Press, 1980.

Hartford, M.E. "Groups in the Human Services: Some Facts and Fancies." *Social Work with Groups,* 19798, 1 (1), pp. 7-13.

Karp, I. "Study On Group Work in a Generic Curriculum." Unpublished.

Lang, N. "A Broad Range Model of Practice in the Social Work Group," in Klenk & Ryan. (Eds.) *The Practice of Social Work.* California: Wadsworth, 1974.

Lee, J.A.B. "Promoting Competence in Children and Youth." In A. Maluccio. (Ed.) *Promoting Competence in Clients: A New/Old Approach to Social Work Practice.* New York: The Free Press, 1980, 236-263.

Lee, J.A.B. & Park, D.N. "A Group Approach to the Depressed Adolescent Girl in Foster Care." *The American Journal of Orthopsychiatry,* 1978, 48(3), pp. 516-527.

Lee, J.A.B. & Swenson, C.R. "Theory in Action: A Community Service Agency." *Social Casework,* 1978, 59(3), pp. 359-370.

Middleman, R. Returning group process to group work. *Social Work with Groups, 1*(1), Spring 1978, pp. 15-26.

Papell, C.P. & Rothman, B. "Relating the Mainstream Model of Social Work with Groups to Group Psychotherapy and the Structured Group Approach." *Social Work with Groups,* Summer, 1980.

Reynolds, B.C. *Learning and Teaching in the Practice of Social Work.* New York: Russell, 1942.

Schwartz, W. "Group Work and the Social Scene." In A. Kahn *Issues in American Social Work.* New York: 1959, pp. 110-137.

Schwartz, W. & Zalba, S. *The Practice of Group Work.* New York: Columbia University, 1971.

Shulman, L. *The Skills of Helping Individuals and Groups.* Itasca, Ill., The Free Press, 1979.

Smalley, R. *Theory for Social Work Practice.* New York: Columbia University Press, 1969.

Swenson, C.R. "Promoting Competence in Social Networks." In A. Malucio. (Ed.) *Promoting Competence in Clients: A New/Old Approach to Social Work Practice.* New York: The Free Press, 1980.

Trecker, H.B. *Group Work: Foundations and Frontiers.* Practitioner's Press, 1955.

Tropp, E. "Whatever Happened to Social Group Work?" *Social Work with Groups,* 1976, 1(1).

Tropp, E. "Three Problematic Concepts: Client, Worker, Help." *Social Caseworker.*

Weiner, H.J. "Social Work Practice in Industrial Social Welfare," Audio Tapes. Columbia University School of Social Work, compiled in 1981.

Woodroofe, K. *From Charity to Social Work.* London: Routledge & Kegan Paul, 1966.

The Dynamics of Mutual Aid

Lawrence Shulman

Of the many contributions Schwartz has made to the group work field, none has been as important as his conceptualization of social work groups as enterprises in mutual aid.[1] Mutual aid had been an element in our early group work literature, however, it was not as clearly defined as central to social work groups until Schwartz gave it an important place in his early work on the mediating (now called interactionist) model. In developing social group work models, theorists and practioners drew from a wide range of professional approaches (e.g., group therapy, social goals orientation, behavioral, educational).[2] For Schwartz, however, the unique role of the social work profession, with its beliefs in self-determination, starting where the client is, reaching for clients strengths, etc., lent itself nicely to a conceptualization of groups in which we helped people to help each other.

This view of a group as a system for mutual aid is rooted in a broader conception of the nature of the relationship between people and society. Schwartz, drawing upon the ideas of Dewey, Mead, Kropotkin, and others, postulated a view of reciprocity between individuals and their social surround.[3] The central idea, as proposed by Schwartz, is that of a "symbiotic" relationship between the individual and societal needs, ". . . each needs the other for its own life and growth and reaches out to the other with all possible strength at a given moment."[4] Schwartz perceived the individual to have a natural impetus toward health and growth and belonging, with a similar impetus on the part of society to integrate its parts into a productive and dynamic whole.

If one then considers the small group to be a special case of this larger individual-social engagement, and one carries this notion of symbiosis into the small group encounter, then Schwartz's definition of a social work group logically follows:

Lawrence Shulman is Professor at the School of Social Work, University of British Columbia, Vancouver, British Columbia.

© 1986 by The Haworth Press, Inc. All rights reserved.

> The group is an enterprise in mutual aid, an alliance of individuals who need each other, in varying degrees, to work on certain common problems. The important fact is that this is a helping system in which the clients need each other as well as the worker. This need to use each other, to create not one but many helping relationships, is a vital ingredient of the group process and constitutes a common need over and above the specific tasks for which the group was formed.[5]

This conceptualization of the group as a mutual aid system had profound implications for the role of the social worker leading the group. Rather than seeing one's sole role as providing help to clients within a group context, the worker would concentrate on the tasks involved in strengthening the members' ability to help each other. The worker, in this view, is but one source of help to clients. This conceptualization helped to solve a number of dilemmas with which group workers continually struggled. For example, would the leader focus on the individual with the problem (the one) or deal with the group (the many). With a mutual aid model in mind, the dichotomy is revealed to be a false one as the group leader concentrates on finding the connections between the individual and the group. As the group members help the individual with a specific problem, they are often also helping themselves with their own similar concerns. In order to see this process more clearly, it is helpful to have some specific ideas about how mutual aid actually works. In what ways can people who are struggling with similar issues actually help each other? The balance of this article addresses this question.

There are a number of mutual aid processes which can be identified when one watches an effective small group in action. These have been described in some detail elsewhere.[6] The nine processes briefly described in this paper include the following: sharing data; the dialectical process; entering taboo areas; the ''all in the same boat'' phenomenon; mutual support; mutual demand; individual problem solving; rehearsal; and the strength in numbers phenomenon.

Sharing Data

In sharing data, group members are able to provide each other with ideas, facts, beliefs, resources, etc., which they have found helpful in coping with similar problems. For example, in a welfare mothers' group, group members had suggestions for how to use the rules of the system to make maximum use of available benefits as well as what places to shop for the best buys. In a married couples group, the older couples could often share their earlier experiences in their marriages, some of which were similar to current crises experienced by the younger couples. The knowledge that the issues were universal and the suggestions as to how to deal with them were often most helpful. While the content of the data varies according to the group type, the essential idea is that people facing similar problems can often be a resource for each other.

The Dialectical Process

The dialectical process consists of one or more members advancing a thesis, other members countering with an antithesis, and the group members attempting to develop their own synthesis. This form of disputation process can be very helpful as one tries to develop insights into difficult problems. A group member can put forth a tentative idea (often only after the worker has helped the group develop a culture of trust and respect) and have other members respond as sounding boards to the views. Other members may change their minds and be open to new ideas as they listen to a view being challenged. One extremely interesting process to observe in a group is the way in which the group may encourage a debate between two members, or two sub-groups, in which each side appears to take an opposing view to the other. For example, in a parents of teenagers group, one side argued impressively for the need to be "tough" and to set limits. The other argued just as passionately for the importance of providing support and of being able to communicate. The apparent dichotomy is, of course, a false one, with the skillful parent learning early of the need to integrate both support and limits at precisely the same time. In fact, each parent carries out internally the same dialogue trying to find a way of resolving the split. In the group, one part of each parent's ambivalence may be assigned to an individual group member of sub-group, and the dialectical process becomes a public airing of each individuals private confusion.

Of course, the assignments are not made consciously. A pre-meeting was not held for the purpose of deciding which group member would articulate which view. This group process emerges from the group's need to articulate and resolve an apparent schism, while simultaneously maintaining the split to avoid having to face it. Bion, in his pioneering work on group processes, observed the way in which immature groups often go into "flight" (changing the subject) or "fight" (strenuous debates and personal attacks) when faced with difficult or frightening issues.[7] He described the group leader's job as pointing out the process and educating the group on its way of working to aid it in becoming a more mature group. In the model suggested here, the worker could identify the common ground, even at the point of conflict, by articulating the part of each group member which really agreed with the "other side." For example: "You're all arguing your points so strenuously, yet I can't believe that some part of each of you isn't struggling to find a way to put together your love for your child with your sense of the importance of setting some limits and providing some structure."

Exploring Taboo Subjects

A third area of mutual aid involves the help members can give each other in discussing a taboo subject. For example, while all group members in my married couples' group may have some issues related to their sexual relationships, they also may experience discussing this subject as taboo. An unstated norm of behavior exists in our society which forbids honest discussion of our fears and concerns in this area. We can joke about such subjects, but real talk is forbidden. Since the sense of urgency about dealing with the subject may be stronger for some couples than others, and/or the fear of discussion may be less powerful, one couple may take the initiative and lead the group into the formerly forbidden area. As group members listen to the discussion, and they see the courageous members supported and credited (often by the leader but just as often by other members), they find their own courage to participate.

In another example of this process in action, some group members may not be in touch with their own feelings if they believe these feelings to be inappropriate (e.g., a parent of a handicapped child who feels anger at the child and the burden he or she represents). As these members hear others speak the unspeakable, it may cause them to experience openly the same emotions.

The "All in the Same Boat" Phenomenon

The mutual experiencing of ideas and emotions leads to yet another powerful mutual aid process: the "all in the same boat phenomenon.'' This is the healing process which occurs when one realizes that one is not alone and that others share the problem, the feelings, the doubts, etc. Students learning to practice social work are greatly relieved to find that other beginning students also wonder if they are right for the field. Parents who experience ''improper'' thoughts and feelings judge themselves less harshly when they find they are not alone.

Emotional Support

A fifth mutual aid process can be observed in the way in which group members provide support for each other. When a group member is in difficulty, or has experienced a trauma (e.g., death in the family), or is revealing painful feelings which have been long repressed, one can see direct and indirect efforts on the part of individual group members and the group-as-a-whole to provide empathic support. Carrying a burden is often easier if others express their understanding. Having peers try to share in your painful feelings can be experienced as a form of a ''gift'', much more meaningful than artificial efforts to cheer you up. In a single parents group, one member began to cry with deep and heartfelt sobs as she described her tremendous sense of rejection by her ex-spouse. The leader could see the member next to the one in distress fidgeting and turning, apparently wanting to reach out. When the leader commented on this and asked if she wanted to hold the women next to her, she replied that she did and then took her hand. This was a physical comforting which was followed by words of support by the other group members. As they were supporting this member in her feelings of rejection, they were also helping themselves with their own similar feelings. Thus, the giving of empathic support is often as helpful to the one who gives as the one who receives. In the small group, the support of peers can be even more powerful in its healing potential than the support of the worker.

Mutual Demand

While support is a crucial ingredient for mutual aid to take place, it is not enough by itself. The change process requires mutual demand as well. It is not unusual to observe groups in which the group members are more ready than the worker to confront each other. The worker may hesitate, concerned about the member's possible fragility, and then sit back in wonder as the "fragile" member responds with strength to the peer groups' demands. Somehow, it is easier to accept a confrontation from one who really knows what it is like than from an "outsider," however caring and empathic. Group members who share the problem may also be more astute in picking up the defenses, the denials, the many ways in which we all "con" ourselves out of facing the truth when it is painful. They are astute observers of these methods of avoidance because they can see them in their own behaviors.

Mutual Expectations

Another simple, yet powerful way in which mutual demand operates in a group, can be the expectation felt by the member that he or she take some difficult action. For example, a men's group discusses a member's difficulty communicating with his boss at work, and after support, discussion, even role play of how he should handle the conversation on the job, the group members expect to hear what happened when they return the next week. Group members have said they would rather face the boss than have to return the following week and reveal to their peers that they "chickened out."

Helping With Specific Problems

While group members can help each other through general discussion of common themes of concern, such as, the feelings of loneliness of a single parent coupled with the fear of risking being hurt again in a new relationship, they must also offer help on a member by member, specific example by specific example basis. In fact, effective mutual aid groups are constantly moving back and forth between the specific case and the general issue. Individual problem solving is one of the important ways a mutual aid group works. As the group members help the individual with a specific problem, they are actually also helping themselves with their own variations on a theme. Workers who are unclear about this specific-general interaction, often make the mistake of keeping the discussion on an overly general level. They express fears of ". . . doing casework in the group." If one is clear that a mutual aid group involves members helping each other, and that there is usually a connection between the individual's specific problem, and the group's general purpose, then this issue of the individual need versus the group's need is revealed as yet another artificial dichotomy.

Take the example of a parents group discussing the difficulty in raising teenage children. One member raises it at the start of a group meeting as follows: "I have been thinking, recently, about how hard it is to raise teenage girls these days, what with the changes taking place in ideas about morality. It just isn't as clear as it was when I was a kid." The group leader who fears "casework in the group" might turn to the other members and ask for their comments on the issue. The resultant general discussion can be become an "illusion of work," and meanwhile, the initiator of the conversation may be sitting there still churning away over the fight she had the night before with her fifteen year old when she didn't return home until 3:30 in the morning.

If the leader is clear about the individual problem solving process in mutual aid groups, he or she might ask the mother if she had a specific incident in mind. As the mother described the fight, the worker would help the mother share the incident with the other group members, invest the presentation with feelings, describe the actual conversation with the daughter, and mobilize the group members to offer feedback and advice. As they discuss this particular parent trying to cope with changing morals and parental responsibility, they will move back and forth between the specific problem and the general issues. As the group members offer help to this mother, they will be formulating new ideas for how they can handle similiar issues with their children.

Rehearsal

Rehearsal has been mentioned in an earlier illustration in this paper; however, it deserves some attention by itself. If one thinks of the group session as having a beginning, middle (or work), and transition and ending phase, then rehearsal can be an extremely effective process as part of the group session ending process. After the issues have been identified in the beginning phase, worked on in the middle phase, then what remains is the task of helping the group member prepare to implement what he or she has taken from the discussion.

If we return to the previous example of the mother with the teenage daughter, discussion of the interaction with the daughter may reveal that the mother was so distraught and worried about her daughter's safety, that she may have translated that concern into an outburst of anger when the daughter returned. While the anger may have been appropriate, it often covers over the fear, anxiety and caring from which it springs. If the group members and the leader help the mother see how she needs to share these feelings as well, then rehearsal, a form of role play in the group, can help the mother find the words and feelings for a follow-up discussion with her daughter. Sometimes, just practicing a difficult task, with support and advice from the group members, can give the member enough confidence to attempt it. In addition, as the member struggles through the role play, he or she often reveals ambivalent feelings about the issue which were not present during the discussion. For example, does some part of the mother not want to have such a discussion with the daughter because she is afraid of what she might hear? It is better if the ambivalence emerges in the group, where it can be explored, rather than in the conversation at home.

Strength in Numbers Phenomenon

Finally, there is the strength in numbers phenomenon. Individual members often feel powerless to deal with large institutions and agencies, helping professionals (even the group leader), and apparently overwhelming tasks. In unity, however, one often finds strength. Take, for example, a group of welfare mothers living in a public housing development in which the management is insensitive to their needs, exploitative (e.g., excessive charges for repairs), and authoritarian (e.g., threatening to evict them if they "make trouble"). For such a group, the idea of confronting the management, dealing with city hall if they meet resistance, in other words, standing up for their rights, can be frightening and risky. In one such group, they faced the additional problem of fear of reprisals from youth gangs in the project if they complained about the drug use in the halls, the welfare checks stolen from their mailboxes, and their general sense of lack of security.[8] It was only through patient work by the group leader, a willingness to recognize the fears lurking beneath the surface, that these group members were able to find the strength in numbers which allowed them to take a small first step.

Conclusion

This paper has described a number of mutual aid processes that can be observed in a group. Of course, these will not necessarily happen by themselves. In fact, it is the difficulty for most groups in learning how to release these powerful forces for change and growth that creates the need for the group worker. While the *potential* for mutual aid is present in the group, it takes hard work by the group leader and all of its members if it is to emerge. There are many delicate moments in which the ability of the group member to take help, and the ability of the group to provide help seems to lie in the balance. For example, group members will be struggling with feelings and ideas about which they may feel ashamed. "I am that handicapped child's mother! How can I feel such strong feelings of hatred towards my own child?"

Strong societal taboos, injunctions against which declare some areas of discussion (e.g., sexual issues), or some feelings as out of bounds, operate to prevent us from honest discussion. These taboos will be brought from the broader society and erected in the microcosim of the small group society. As the small group gingerly approaches the taboo area, employing indirect communications such as "hints", the worker will have to call the group members attention to the barrier and assist them in dealing with it, through a combination of support and demand. The members, for their part, will have to find the courage to enter the formerly forbidden areas, in response to the workers' gentle pushing, and begin to discover they are "all in the same boat." The feelings for which they judged themselves so harshly, are normal for their situations. The subjects they felt were not for open discussion, the feelings they experienced as possibly too painful to be faced, all of these take on a managable status as the healing power of mutual aid begins its work.

It is beyond the scope of this paper to discuss all of the obstacles and the ways in which the group leader can intervene to help. The crucial point, for now, is to recognize the power and potential of mutual aid in groups.

REFERENCE NOTES

1. For his seminal work on the mutual aid model, see: William Schwartz, "The Social Worker in the Group," in *New Perspectives on Services to Groups: Theory, Organization and Practice* (New York: National Association of Social Workers, 1961), pp. 7-34; and The *Social Welfare Forum, 1961* (New York: Columbia University Press, 1961), pp. 146-77. See also: Lawrence Shulman, *The Skills of Helping Individuals and Groups, 2nd Edition* (Itasca, Illinois: F.E. Peacock, Publishers, 1984).

2. For an early article identifying the emergence of different models of group work practice, see: Catherine P. Papell & Beula Rothman, "Social Groupwork Models: Possession and Heritage." *Journal of Education for Social Work 2 (2): 66-77.*

3. Schwartz, "The Social Worker in the Group." See also: Peter Kropotkin, *Mutual Aid: A Factor of Evolution* (New York: Alfred A. Knopf, 1925); George Herbert Mead, *Mind, Self and Society* (Chicago: University of Chicago Press, 1934).

4. Schwartz, "The Social Worker in the Group," pg. 15.

5. Ibid., p. 19.

6. Shulman, "The Skills of Helping Individuals and Groups." Chapter 7. For illustrative examples of the mutual aid process in a number of different settings, with different age groups, see also: Alex Gitterman & Lawrence Shulman, eds. *Mutual Aid Groups and the Life Cycle* (Itasca, Ill.: F.E. Peacock, Publishers, Inc., 1985).

7. William R. Bion, *Experiences in Groups* (New York: Basic Books, 1961).

8. Lawrence Shulman, *The Skills of Helping Individuals and Groups, 2nd Edition,* pp. 385-90.

Busted and Branded: Group Work with Substance Abusing Adolescents in Schools

Sally Ann Shields

Adolescent substance abusers are frequently described as a resistant hard-to-reach population significantly different from their non-substance using counterparts. This view often creates a mystique surrounding group work with these adolescents and results in efforts to remove such youngsters from the general population in the school they are identified. It is true that research on adolescent substance users has indicated a constellation of personality traits and school variables significantly different in substance users from non-users. Alienation and rebelliousness (Steffenhagen, Polich, and Lash, 1978, Smith and Fogg, 1979, McCorry, 1982), high school maladjustment (Halikas and Rimmer, 1974), and diminished interest in school and academic recognition (Jessor, Jessor, and Finney, 1973) are some. Moreover, the primary role of the peer group in supporting the substance using behavior is well documented (Kandel, 1974, Kandel, Treiman, and Faust, and Single, 1976). An alienated, rebellious youth, whose friends support and encourage his/her drug use and who seems to find little meaning or value in the educational process would seem a poor risk for a school-based counseling service.

The New York Archdiocese Drug Abuse Prevention Program's (ADAPP)* experience with the drug abusing high school student over the past decade bears out the existence of the general characteristics of alientation, rebelliousness, and school problems, as described in the research. However, to understand why these students present themselves in this way, a closer examination of the needs

*ADAPP is a program of the Superintendent's Office of the Department of Education of the Archdiocese of New York. The program in existence since 1972 is funded by the New York State Division of Substance Abuse Services (DSAS). ADAPP provides services in elementary and secondary schools in ten counties of New York State.

© 1986 by The Haworth Press, Inc. All rights reserved.

and perceptions of this population is required. All the students participating in the groups described in this paper were referred primarily for substance use by school authorities. In all cases, other problems were identified as well, such as multiple academic failures, running away, truancy and/or parental alcoholism. Over and above the manifest traits described in the literature, which these secondarily identified reasons for referral seem to bear out, the most common dynamics exhibited by these students is a pattern of avoidance and the absence of effective problem-solving skills. Generally, these students present a facade of toughness, mistrust and hostility which tends to keep others, both peers and adults, at a distance. However, beneath this facade, often lurks an extremely vulnerable, frightened and overwhelmed adolescent at a loss of how to cope with himslef and his world. Torn between the normal adolescent strivings toward autonomy and a need for dependency, these adolescents seem to choose an exaggerated posture of independence not only toward adults but toward their peers as well. With a shrug of the shoulders and the phrase, "I really don't care anyway," this adolescent can be seen walking away from home, from school and even from friends. This avoidance, at best, serves the need of the adolescent for control and, at worst, futher isolates him from those systems from which he both needs and wants nurturance, acceptance, and support. When avoidance is impossible because of the nature of the situation or the intensity of the feeling, this same adolescent can become verbally and/or physically aggressive with often the same resulting isolation, and overwhelming feeling of inadequacy, sadness and anxiety.

Painful feelings may be warded off at least temporarily through the use of drugs and alcohol. Substance use becomes a means of coping with environmental and psychological stress. Unsuccessful in gaining acceptance in the conventional and socially acceptable way, the drug using adolescent becomes involved with a fringe peer group built around their drug using behaviors, common isolation and stigmatized status. This creates then, the appearance of such traits as alienation, rebelliousness, and resistance as previously noted. It is our clinical experience that it is not an absence of motivation that isolates these youngsters so much as their inability to recognize their stake in their nuturing systems and reach out to them for help effectively, whether that system be the school, the family or the peer group. The substance abusing students do not, in this author's experience, differ from their non-drug using counterparts in their intelligence or aspirations for success, acceptance, and recognition, though these may be deeply buried by an armor of protective defenses. The subtance using students do, however, appear unable to sustain the challenge and continuous effort needed to resolve complex social and academic tasks involving accurate perception, understanding, analysis, judgement, and decision making. Why they lack these problem-solving skills at this point in their lives is not the issue here but rather, it is how to help such adolescents develop the coping skills necessary to lead more productive life styles within the mainstream of society.

By employing a model of group work that emphasizes viewing the client in interaction with his relevant systems, in this case the schools, intervention with the substance abusing adolescent proceeds at several levels. The work of William Schwartz offers such a framework in his development of the Mutual Aid Model.[1] It is precisely at the point where the relationship between the adolescent and his nurturing system has become blocked and obscured that the social worker defines his function. With the Mutual Aid Model, the worker is a third party assisting the individual and the system recognize their stake in each other and helps both reach out to the other in more effective ways (Schwartz, 1961). Through the placement of the adolescent in a different peer group, however temporary, the model takes advantage of the role of peers in supporting ways of behaving among adolescents. The group can create a considerable degree of peer pressure to face reality. A peer group can also offer a multiplicity of helping relationships to the adolescent in the struggle toward health while, at the same time, support the adolescent's striving for autonomy.

Using the group process, the adolescent substance user can learn new ways to deal with old problems—problems that have reinforced his alienation or isolation from the system, heightened stress and confrontation making substance use an attractive means of coping with developmental and environmental tasks through avoidance. At the same time, the school can be helped to recognize and support the adolescents's strivings, and to surrender old perceptions of the individual, as they both move toward a more productive relationship.

The mediating function of the Mutual Aid Model which presupposes a relationship between the individual and his nurturing group, with each needing each other for its own life and growth, clarifies particularly the role of the worker in an institution where the social service is secondary to the goals of the institution. For ADAPP, this is clearly an advantage because it defines the service clearly as one of helping the drug using student or the student considered at high risk of drug use, to use the school more effectively and cope with the developmental issues inherent in the educational experience in adaptive ways, rather than by withdrawal through substance use. Simultaneously, the model requires that the worker help the school reach out to these students more effectively and help the institution create an atmosphere where these students can try out new behaviors. It is this mediating function which helps the worker resist the lure of overidentification with either the needs of the institution or the needs of the individual clients that makes this model so effective to a school-based service.

Another advantage of this model, in addition to its clear definition of function to a large agency such as ADAPP providing services in some 50 schools, is its insistence on skill delineation. Specificity of skill inherently places a high priority on the quality of service delivery and accountability important to any agency but particularly so to a publicly funded program. In this model, method is function in action. The skills of practice can be partialized and documented, so becoming a focus for supervision and in-service training. Thus, the agency is able to unify the talent and training of its professional staff in a systematic approach to a social problem, such as drug abuse. The adoption of a model which is transmissible and evaluable allows an agency to continually examine, refine and replicate its service, building a body of knowledge to draw from in its approach to a particular social problem.

Lastly, the dimension of time is an important component of this model, which is an additional advantage to a school-based service. School life is clearly defined by time segments, the years, the semester, the days. By definition a school-based service is time-limited and the model helps make use of time limits to benefit the delivery of service. Time is used to plan and analyze the work. The tasks and skills of the worker are viewed specifically within the four phases of work and are best understood as the worker moves through each of these phases in sequence. The first is preparatory, a "tuning-in" phase, in which the worker readies himself to enter the process. The second is a "contracting" phase in which the worker helps the group make its beginnings under clear conditions of purpose. The next is the "middle" phase, that period of time encompassing the essential work of the group. This is the time where the needs of the members become the tasks to be addressed and the themes of work emerge. The final period of the group is that of "transitions and endings" when the group concerns itself with the problems of leaving, separation and termination (Schwartz, 1971). Each of these phases can be seen in a single session, as well as over the life of the group. In each phase, there are specific parallel tasks for the worker and the group members, and particular professional skills dominate.

This article will examine the Mutual Aid Model in practice with groups of adolescents mandated to participate in the program by school officials because of known drug use. The group practice of the first three phases of the group will be detailed to illustrate, in particular, the processes of preparatory tuning-in, initial contracting, and some of the dominant themes that emerge in the work phase with substance-using adolescents in a school-based group counseling program.

The Tuning-In

According to Schwartz, in the pre-group phase there must be an effort to merge psychological insight with the dimension of purpose. The worker readies him/herself to enter the helping process, to hear cues that are subtle and unspoken. The tuning-in is a multi-level process. The worker must sensitize him/herself to the concerns and issues of the adolescent population and the school in general, and then particularize these concerns to the individuals referred at this time, in this school setting. So, the worker first would consider general adolescent issues (eg., the need to establish a sense of autonomy and independence) as well as, the general concerns of the school (eg., fear of the impact of a drug user on the larger school community and the expectation of an immediate behavior change). After such general considerations, the worker must tap into his own adolescent experiences to evoke the feelings involved at this developmental stage (Shulman, 1979). The worker's next task is to apply the results of this general tuning-in to the specific circumstances of the particular clients he/she is preparing to meet. In a situation where the students were mandated to group for drug problems, a worker might anticipate the anger at school authorities to be directed toward him/her and possibly complicate the ever present authority issues of the group. Denial, which is often a problem in working with substance abusers may be heightened by the circumstances of the referral. Students will no doubt resist the school's spoken and unspoken expectations of counseling as a cure for such "bad behavior." Talking openly about the taboo area of drug use in the school setting will be an issue. If the circumstances of the referral are public knowledge, there also may be a real or perceived stigma attached to these youngsters. The resultant feelings such as anger, shame, embarass-ment, and/or guilt will certainly color the initial encounters with the worker, who may be seen by the students as one more person in a complicated system who intrudes into their private business. However, as in all new situations, there will be ambivalent feelings present in the first encounters with this helping person. In spite of the circumstances, the students will have some hope, however small, that the worker may be able to help them deal with their distressing situation. For them, this distress may not be their use of drugs so much as the trouble they are now in with the school. This trouble may be the felt concern which will be the common element that joins the group together initially and will be the starting point for the work. It is that part of the student that is reaching out to the school, hoping that the situation can be improved, desiring success and recognition that must be tapped by the worker.

As the worker is tuning-in to the students, he/she must also tune-in to the school system. There are two major reasons for this. First, as was indicated above, the school authorities' dealings with the students regarding the referral to group will greatly color the initial group meeting with the worker. If the school has communicated to the student expectations of instant "cures", or if the referral has been made clearly as a disciplinary measure, "maybe a drug counselor can straighten you out, we have given up," additional obstacles will be present initially. Also, such tuning-in to the school system will help the worker determine the scope and focus of their mediating role with the school. There is a great deal of work to be done outside the group. The interactional approach demands that the worker, while helping the individual reach out to the system, in this case the school, is simultaneously assisting the system to reach out to the individual. The assumption at the core of the Mutual Aid Model is that a part of each individual potentially strives toward health and Schwartz applies this to the social system, as well. While the work with the school system is not the concentration of this article, it must be noted that without on-going and effective work with the school on the issues related to substance abuse, no real success with the students can be sustained. Mediation with the school is necessary to reduce the mystique surrounding work with substance abusers, to lessen the stigma placed on individuals referred for help with drug problems, and to identify realistic expectations of the group services. School drug policies that integrate the agency's group service with the philosophy, values and goals of the school must be formulated if the student is to be enabled to talk openly about such a taboo area as drugs in the school setting. Tolerance by the school system to the group program is not sufficient for its success. There must be a recognition on the part of the worker, as well as the school, that these students are ultimately the school's clients; the purpose of the school is education and the worker is there to mediate between the two, helping each to realize the stake they have in each other.

Lastly, tuning-in requires that the workers tune-in to their selves, their responses to the clients' situation, their worries about the first meeting and most particularly, to sort out what kind of help they are offering. Defining that help can present a dilemma to a worker providing services to drug using adolescents, particularly those mandated to group services. The raison d'être for the workers very presence in the school is drug prevention. Yet if the work is defined by the goal, the traps of focusing on individual behavioral change and neglecting the system, of moralizing and attempting to convince or manipulate the adolescent away from drug use, are almost unavoidable and inevitably heighten resistance. Such an approach focuses directly on the defense of drug use, the symptom of the breakdown of the engagement between the individual and his nurturing system, rather than focusing on the student's potential strengths and building on them. The Mutual Aid Model requires the worker to make the insistent demand for work the goal of the helping process. This demand for work is accomplished by the worker's use of professional skills in helping the clients to examine their world in detail, to dig deep into their experiences including their drug use and to help each other find new ways of handling old problems. The work of the group becomes the struggle of each to cope with the very specific problems of daily living. Drug use can be openly examined as one way of coping with the world but other choices are opened up, examined, rehearsed and supported. This does not call for an arbitrary or permissive attitude toward drug use on the part of the worker. Rather, it calls into question the expectation that any one individual can change another. The Model instead requires the use of professional skills targeted toward the development of a mutual aid system in the group which will support, nurture and facilitate the development of adaptive ways of coping on the part of the individual members. The worker, as Schwartz puts it, must be strengthened by the idea that he cannot change anybody; but there is work to be done and his skills can help (Schwartz, 1971). The work then, becomes a real examination of the drug use and what it means to the individual. Ideally, from such tuning in the worker can formulate a proposed contract and also prepare each student individually for the first group meeting.

The Contract

The worker's task in contracting is to help the group make its beginning under clear conditions of work. Schwartz defines the contract as the convergence of two sets of tasks—those of the clients and those of the agency—which create the terms of the contract that is made between the client group and the worker. The contract establishes the frame of reference for the work that will follow. It allows one to understand when the work is progressing, when it is being evaded and when it is completed. A clear connection between the group's needs and the proposed agency service thus provide clarity and direction both for the worker and the group member. The task of the worker in contracting then, is one of making a clear unjargonized statement of purpose which touches the common needs of the group members and of making an offer of service that illustrates the connection between the individual's stake and the agency's stake in the service. Contracting is a tentative process and the worker must reach for the reservations of the members not assuming agreement or interpreting silence for consensus. A contract must be as real to the members as to the worker if it is to define the terms of their engagement in such a way that each can recognize his/her own stake in the process and invest in it wholeheartedly.

The following illustration is taken from a first session of a meeting with six tenth grade girls. Three were reportedly found high on Angel Dust (PCP) in school, one was discovered in possession of marijuana and hashish, and two were reported smoking pot on the bus enroute to school. All the students were seen individually for assessment prior to the group and it was determined that, though all used drugs to varying degrees, none were physically addicted.

> The worker initially introduces the girls.
> Worker: This is what I know—all of you are in trouble here in school because of drugs. The principal has spoken to all your parents and has told them you are all one step from being expelled. (The students all agree). Worker: Now, the principal asked me to meet you. I've been thinking about what I can do to help. I think your drug use, whether a little or a lot, has gotten you in trouble with your families and here in school. Now, I know I can't stop you from getting high, and I'm not going to preach about drugs. You've heard all that. I know you make your own decisions about getting high, but since all of you are facing similar hassles—like probation here in school, feeling everybody is watching you, hassles with your parents, decisions about drugs—I think you can help each other work these things out, and I can help you do that. You've all told me you want to stay in school, and I'd like to help you do that, but it will mean work—looking hard at how you make decisions about getting high in school, how you handle the restrictions of probation and problems that arise with teachers here at school. Now, I think we can work these things out together—I can help you work together on these issues here in group. I can help you talk to teachers and maybe parents or I can even talk to them with you, but you have to be willing to really share and work together here on the hassles you're facing if group is going to help. How about it? Can we do it? (Silence).

Here, the Worker begins the group identifying the common experience of the members vis à vis the school. The statement is simple, direct and designed to let the students know they are all in the same boat. The Worker names some of the common concerns they may be facing as a result of the school's discovery of their drug use but does not assume that the students share a felt concern over their drug use per se. Rather, the Worker starts with the common circumstances of the referral, their expressed desire to remain in the school, and insists that if the group is to be helpful they must be willing to examine their drug use and its consequences, thus defining the work of the group. The group's response is silence. Schwartz identified a skill he called reaching inside the silence. It calls for an exploration of the silent response, precisely because it is a response, to better understand what the client is thinking and feeling at a given moment. Tuning-in can ready the Worker to reach for the meaning of such silences.

> Worker: Now everyone is quiet. Is talking about drugs here in school too hard or just a dumb idea? What do you think? (Laughter) Lisa: Well, it's not like we are all junkies! But, I think I can talk about it. Like yesterday, the Principal actually called me in to look at my eyes. (The group begins to ventilate their complaints and give their side of their stories).

The Worker reaches in the above for the reservations toward the group purpose which may be being expressed by the group silence. The group responds by voicing their complaints about the school (authority) seemingly testing the worker's reactions and possibly determining where she stands relative to the school and them.

> Members talk angrily about being questioned by the Principal. Worker: Well, how about if I ask you questions in the group? Lisa: I don't think it will be the same. Carrie: Who knows, you might agree with them (school). Worker: I might. Jane: Maybe you would say the same stuff as the school, but your job is to understand us. I think it would be different here. (Members then begin to fill each other in on their parents' responses to the school situation).

Initially, the Worker clarifies his/her role in the group further and continues reaching for reservations. The Worker's role within the school and the confidentiality of the group are potential obstacles to the work. These need to be worked and reworked at various times during the life of the group. The students allude to these concerns here. With Carrie and Lisa's responses, he/she seems to miss what could be important cues. The Worker does not reach for specificity in these responses. Carrie's comment, particularly, appears to indicate unspoken concerns about the Worker. She seems to ask if the worker will view her as the school does; but, what that actually means to Carrie is not revealed. A simple question in response to Carrie's comment like, "Agree with the school about what?" might have helped Carrie express how she feels she is viewed by the school and her concerns about the worker. Reaching for the details of Jane's comment, too, would have helped to clarify for the group what the "stuff" is that the school seems to be saying, and more importantly the specifics on how it might be different in group as she sees it. One would wonder if perhaps, the worker, too, is anxious about her identification with the school authority and that this contributed to her missing these cues.

> (As the first session continues the members begin to discuss how both students and faculty are talking about them in school). Jane: It seems like everyone knows I was busted! Worker: It is hard to face coming to school when you feel labeled. (The girls all loudly agree). Worker: This is certainly one of the things we can work on in group—that you can help each other deal with—along with the other hassles you face here at school, at home and with your friends. You've all said you want to stay in this school, so I'd like to help you figure out what you need to do so you can stay. How's that? Joan: My sister dropped out of school. I want to graduate. Lisa: Me too, I've done lots of different drugs but some people can handle it and some can't. I got caught. Carrie: Yeah. (Carrie then tells the others how she got drunk the night of the school incident, so she wouldn't have to think about it. Jane says she did the same thing. Their discussion continues until the session nears its end). Worker: I guess there really is a lot to talk about in terms of school and how you use drugs and alcohol. If you are willing to work, so am I. She notes that the time is almost up, and details when and where they will meet the following week. The first group session ends and the girls leave together.

In the preceding section, the Worker identifies the common feeling of stigma that the group is describing and indicates it as an area for work. Along with this theme of stigmatized status, other areas for future work are pointed out—namely, the hassles they face in school, at home and with peers, along with the decisions they have to make regarding drugs and alcohol. These themes will recur throughout the life of the group. In this way the worker clarifies her offer of service and expectations of the group. The more specific the offer of service, the more the group members have to hold on to and the clearer the boundaries. Thus, less energy has to go into figuring out the worker, testing the boundaries and searching out hidden agendas. Ambiguity creates anxiety which in turn intensifies defensive behavior. It is a common error in group contracting to offer the group as a place to talk, to share feelings or other like general statements, thinking this will create a freer atmosphere. While it is true talking, sharing and expression of feeling all occur in group they do not constitute group purpose. A group forms for specific reasons, and it is the purpose for which the group is formed that defines the work to be done. The group purpose must be clear both to the clients and the worker. This does not negate renegotiation of the contract, testing of limits and so on. These will take place from time to time and should be expected. However, ambiguity of purpose at the onset results in a prolonged dickering about the terms of the engagement and becomes an obstacle to the work (Schwartz, 1971).

In summary, the ambivalent feelings present in this new situation of the group create questions in the clients' mind at the first session such as: "Why am I here?" "Are these others here for the same reasons?" "What is expected of me?" "What can I expect from the worker?" The students described above brought many negative experiences of authority and will have these questions uppermost in their minds. The contracting process can be broken down into three basic elements that address these questions or client concerns. First, the worker touches a common need, identifies a shared concern or experience thus answering the questions, "Why am I here?" and "Are these others in the same boat?" Second, the worker offers a service in response to that common need and clarifies his/her role responding to the questions, "What is this group about?" "What is expected of me?" and "What can I expect from this worker?" Last, the worker reaches for the reservations, the fears and concerns regarding group participation and helps the clients to recognize their stake in the process. Then the work can begin.

The Middle Phase

The Worker during this phase enables the group to become an enterprise in mutual aid, characterized by the alliance of individuals who need each other to work on certain common problems. The group becomes a helping system in which the members need each other as well as the worker. The individual member is offered not one but many helping relationships. The Worker's function remains one of mediation principally clarifying the contract and maintaining a demand for work. The attention of the Worker in the Middle Phase focuses on helping the members work things out together.

The practice skills which facilitate this work include: helping break down large problems into more manageable pieces; responding to covert cues, reaching for feeling along with content; helping members dig deeply into their experience; rehearsing new ways of handling old problems; and helping the members listen to and support each other. Above all, it is the Worker's task to guard the focus of the work, to point out obstacles when they arise and to invest his/her own compassion and spontaneity without losing the helping role (Schwartz, 1961).

In school substance abuse groups, as with other groups, the themes of authority and intimacy in their many forms dominate this phase of group life. These themes emerge from the work as the students tackle their problems with drugs, school, parents and peers. A review of a limited number of ADAPP substance abuse groups, similar to the one used to illustrate the Beginning Phase, reveals some common patterns in the Middle Phase. The issues of trust, labeling and authority conflicts recurred throughout each group. Problems of communication with authority figures and peers were evident as the groups worked on the drug theme. The issue of occupying a stigmatized status was a particularly strong common concern and constituted another predominant work theme. Confidentiality and trust within the group became an internal working through of the authority/intimacy conflict as it moved into taboo areas. As in other groups, these members concerned themselves with resolving their relationship to this Worker who was both a nurturing and demanding authority figure. A discussion of the themes of drug use and stigmatized status with record excerpts follows, illustrating how these groups worked during the Middle Phase.

The Drug Theme

A study of a number of these groups indicated that work on the drug theme typically underwent various transitions. Initially, in these groups there was a good deal of denial and this necessitated continued work on the contract. This work consisted of the Worker's ongoing insistence on the examination of the reality of the students' school probation due to involvement with drugs. As the denial and externalization diminished, the actual work on the drug theme began. In the beginning this work was largely cognitive. The students discussed issues regarding drugs, asked for information, exchanged data and at times shared "war" stories. There seemed to be an attempt on their part to understand and test out ideas about substance use while remaining somewhat distant. The Worker's reactions were watched carefully as the members tested the "waters" tentatively using, for example, a movie or a third person as a vehicle for the talk. If the experiences were personal, they were shared in the past tense and with little affect. With the Worker's help, the group moved from this type of general talk to examining their specific concerns about drugs. The talk became more serious and invested with feeling. Members began sharing their own troubles and formerly concealed worries about their use of substances both in and out of school. There were expressions of shame, anger and embarrassment as they shared their stories. Talking with feeling became the norm and group support and mutual aid the moving force.

In this third session of a group of seven high school Senior boys, the Worker attempts to intrude into the members' somewhat bravado attitude and move the group toward more serious work on the drug theme.

> (The boys began the group by joking and fooling about their marjuana use). Worker: For the past two weeks we've talked about problems connected to getting high in school, maybe you could tell me some of the good parts? (The group is thrown off balance by the question and the members look perplexed). Andy: What do you mean? The benefits? Worker: Yes, like what do you personally get out of it? Dan: You mean why? Ron: Well, music sounds better—I have more fun. Jim: Yeah, you have a better time. (All agree). Larry: (hesitantly) I haven't smoked in two weeks. Richie: Me either. (Members start joking and teasing each other). Worker: (asks Richie and Larry) How come you haven't smoked? Larry: I had no money. Richie: I got drunk instead. Worker: Oh, that doesn't count? Richie: No, it's different. (The group laughs). Dan: Oh, come off it Rich, it's no different. Richie: I think it is. Worker: How is it different for you? Richie: Well, I don't worry about it. (pause) Like sometimes I'm afraid I smoke too much. I'll become a burn out. Carl: Sometimes, I don't even want to do it. But I do. Larry: It's something to look forward to. Tim: Like on a nice day like today—you get stoned outside—it's real nice. Carl: I wouldn't. Tim: Why not? Carl: It's too nice out. Dan: I would, just to relax. I'm so tense after school! Worker: What do you mean tense? (Dan begins to talk about the

pressure he feels in school. He shares with the group that he is worried he won't graduate and how ashamed his parents will be. The others listen intently). Worker: Does anyone else feel discouraged and worried about graduating? (Others share their particular concerns, and a discussion ensues about the particular pressures of senior year and the weight of future decisions).

In the record excerpt, the Worker is predominately employing elaborating skills. The group is helped to move from the general to specific through interventions aimed at partialization. The Worker's skill in reaching for details enables the group to focus and begin to share from personal experiences. Additionally, the Worker seeks to create a climate where "real" talk about drugs can take place. This is evident in the Worker's initial question and her genuine curiousity about their experiences. Often, the expectation of the students is that adults will only accept what they want to hear and that is the negative aspect of substance use. Opening up such a taboo area as the perceived benefits of drug use reflects the Worker's attempt to enable the students to tackle this question realistically from all angles.

As the end of the school year approached, the groups were closely examining the role drugs play in their lives. In some groups. the students began to anticipate when drugs might cause them trouble. They began discussing what, when and how much substances they might use in a given situation, as opposed to their former indiscriminate multi-substance use. Additionally, some members expressed feelings of reservation with such comments as, "It's not much fun anymore because I think about it now." Others verbalized a new caution and awareness of certain previously used substances. In a large number of instances, members began to use the group for support by reporting their efforts at cutting down and abstinence. These students would often report anticipated situations where they would feel a need to get high. The group then was used to examine such a situation closely and work through associated feelings, possibly coming up with new ways of handling the particular situation.

In the eighth session of an all girls group of Juniors and Seniors, one girl Jean talks about a new boy she has met. The group begins to discuss how Jean can let this boy know she likes him.

Jean: I think I'd have to be high to tell him I like him. Worker: How high? Jean: Maybe just two drinks. I don't know.

Worker: How come, you think? Chris: I know what she is saying. Jean: Just to be relaxed. Worker: You are scared to talk to him? Jean: Yeah, I'm real nervous. (Others agreed saying they have been in similar situations). Worker: What about it makes you nervous? Jean: I don't think he gets high. He goes home early. I think he gets along with his parents good. He's still fun! I really want to get to know a guy like that. His parents are strict. Worker: You really sound like you want to get to know what it's like to stay straight, get along at home and still have fun. Jean: I think being with people like that would help me. I haven't been high—on anything—in at least 4 weeks. I was even offered dust and didn't take it. (Silence) Worker: You look like you are thinking hard. Can you tell us what's going on in your head. Jean: Well, here I am so proud that I've been straight—the longest time in a couple of years—it's probably crazy to say I need to get high to talk to him. I really don't want to. . . Worker: It's not crazy. On the one hand it seems like a solution to get high so you won't be nervous, but on the other hand part of you wants to do without getting high. Jean: Yeah, I don't know, maybe, I could do it on my own. Worker: But you are not sure? Jean: Yes, I'm sure I want to talk to him. I'm sure I'd rather be straight, but I know I'd be nervous. Chris: So, you'll be nervous. Carrie: I bet he'll be more nervous. I never thought guys got nervous asking girls, but they do. (This discussion continues, and later in the session the group begins to use role play to get closer to the experience and share ideas on how to handle it).

In the above excerpt, the work on the drug theme becomes part of the work on coping with normal adolescent developmental issues. Substance use as a coping mechanism is clearly illustrated. As the members struggle with their concerns and how to deal with the anxiety of social situations it is imperative for the Worker to be tuned in to the adolescent experience. Only with such tuning in can the Worker help the group work together to find their own answers. In the above the Worker helps Jean put her struggle into words, and this allows the others to identify with the problem. The Worker moves slowly, reaching inside the silences for the unspoken ambivalences. She/he doesn't succumb to a premature consideration of alternatives or false reassurances. Clearly, the Worker is attempting to bring Jean and the group closer to the experience in their search for their own unique answers. A non-judgemental attitude is demonstrated not only toward the negative but the positive as well when Jean shares that she hasn't been high in four weeks. Rather than offer praise at this point, the Worker responds to the silence acting on the hunch that something important has been left unsaid. This frees Jean to continue to share her conflicting feelings.

Stigmatized Status Theme

Another recurrent theme that emerges in substance abuse groups during the Work Phase is that of the members' perception of their stigmatized status. This theme is not isolated to the youngsters' feeling labeled in school but often extends to their perception of their negative status within the family and among their peers. The painful feelings of rejection by such vital support systems are usually buried beneath the substance abusers' "cool" and "with-it" image. It is the facade of toughness, mistrust and an exaggerated posture of independence that protects these youngsters from their own neediness and vulnerability. This theme dramatically points to the obstacles that have obscured the connection between these adolescents and the nurturing systems they desperately need as resources for growth and development. Real or imagined, the stigma felt by them can become a self-fulfilling prophesy. In their attempt to ward off the pain of isolation, the adolescent externalizes the problem and rejects the system often by increasing his/her withdrawal and/or acting out. This behavior serves to reinforce the substance abuser's label as a hard to reach, resistant and alienated individual. Whether the stigma is real or projected is not the issue. As has been said previously, the Worker's role is defined precisely at that point the relationship between the individual and the system has become blocked. Here, then, the first task of the Worker is to help the group members go beyond the externalizations and reactive behaviors in order to experience their pain and rediscover their stake in the system. Initially, this work often involves a good deal of ventilation and anger. It is very tempting to push toward solutions. Premature offers of solutions to this problem are doomed to failure or worse create the illusion that the youngster need only to manipulate the system more effectively and the problem will be solved, i.e., people will be off their backs. Additionally, such moves communicate a lack of understanding to the adolescents of their problem and/or the Worker may be perceived as blaming them for their problems. It is, therefore, imperative that the Worker focus his/her efforts on helping the group move beyond the externalization slowly, reaching for the feelings beneath the anger and for the hope that change is possible. The Worker must be sensitized by his/her own need to cope with the complexities of living and growing and from that fund of feeling draw his/her attempts to understand the members' struggles. This understanding is communicated in the ability to empathize precisely with the feelings engendered in the group member by the demands of a particular situation. The Workers need to call up parts of their own life experiences, to communicate feelings, and to demonstrate an active faith in the productive capacities of the individual (Schwartz, 1961). The purpose is to reach the underlying and unexpressed feelings that accompany the content and then help the member(s) work through the pain in the here-and-now experience of the group. Without a deep sense of empathy, attempts at reaching the affective component of the work tend to become rote and routinized. Questions like, "How did you feel about that?" indicate a distance between the Worker and the group and may serve to divorce the feeling from the experience.

Work on the Stimatized Status Theme, as with other work themes in the Middle Phase, must be characterized by an intense flow of affect between the Worker and the members. The Worker's feeling involvement demonstrates his/her conviction that the process of growing is complex and difficult but also rewarding and possible. Expression of affect is essential to the work. The group process is not a panacea, member and worker must invest his/her heart and mind in the process (Schwartz, 1966).

The following practice excerpt illustrates the Worker helping the group get closer to their subjective experience of feeling labeled and stigmatized. It is a beginning of the work on this theme and necessary to help the adolescents rediscover their stake in the system.

> (As the group begins Jane is telling the others how a friend passed her on the street and wouldn't speak to her). Jane: But that is cool. It's her choice. (Silence) Worker: You don't look like it's cool. You look real sad? Jane: No, it's cool. Pauses. Jane starts to tell the group how she can't believe friends can do things like that to each other, and she begins to cry. Jane: I can't talk about this—it makes me cry. Worker: Can you keep talking while you cry so we can all know what you are going

> through? Jane: (crying) I guess her mother told her I'm a bad influence or something. I think I really have it hard. Worker: What do you mean? Jane: (hesitantly) I stayed here in the same school and neighborhood and tried to stop doing drugs, but nobody cares, not even the school! Lisa: Yeah, it's easy for those kids who go away. I know what you mean about the school. Joan: I think they think we are bad for the other kids. Sue: Yeah, and we are here, and the others are out getting high. What a joke! Jane: I don't care what the Principal thinks, I didn't do drugs this whole weekend, and it's the third week I didn't get high in school. Worker: You sound proud of yourself. Is it hard when you are working so hard and feel others still suspect you? Lisa: I don't let it bother me. Carrie: People here still call me "Dusthead". I wish the Principal wouldn't act so suspicious. It makes me want to get high. Lisa: Yeah. I hate it. I say it doesn't bother me, but it does. (Silence) Worker: Lisa you look like you are thinking hard. Can you think out loud? Lisa: I was thinking that I just admitted it really bothers me that the Principal thinks I'm no good. If I said anything to her I'd probably get mad and get in more trouble. Jane: I'd be too scared to try to talk to her. I can't even talk to my mother. It doesn't come out right; then we end up fighting. Carrie: I don't get scared. I get mad. All they do is pick, pick, pick,—it's no wonder we get high just so we don't have to listen. I just go in my own little world. Jane: Yeah, that's what I used to do, but I don't want that anymore. Worker: Don't want what? Jane: I want people to know I'm different now. But I don't know how.

Empathetic to the adolescent experience, the Worker in the above record picks up Jane's concern and the work theme of stigmatized status emerges from the concern of this individual member. As Jane begins to talk she can no longer contain her feelings of anger and sadness. The Worker helps her continue by inviting her to go on through her tears. Jane does this and helps the other members get closer to their own feelings of isolation and pain. In this illustration the individual was reaching out to the group indirectly through what could be interpreted mistakenly as small talk as the group was settling down for the session. Unless a Worker is tuned in to such potential concerns, they are easily missed opportunities. The acceptance expressed by the Worker freed the individual to drop some of the control and released a valuable source of energy. Seeing a youngster in pain should be a heart wrenching experience, but it should not drive a worker to close off the pain by false reassurances and easy solutions. The pain must be lived through, and the group should be a safe and accepting environment in which to do so. Schwartz insists that instead of teaching clients to talk about feelings Social Workers help clients to talk with feeling. When Jane began to cry, the Worker here resisted the natural urge to point out that she had other friends, or allow her to withdraw into her pain. Instead, this worker helped Jane get her story out with feeling realizing that the only thing worse than living with strong emotions is the feeling that one is alone with them because others don't understand.

Later, as the work on this theme of stigmatized status evolves, the group will be ready to focus on problem-solving, examining options and rehearsing new ways of dealing with the problem. Role play can be an important tool in helping the group get close to their experiences of the intricacies of communication. Work on communication skills is an important area in the work on this theme as the inability to communicate with authority is often a common obstacle and source of tension that contributes to the breakdown between the adolescent and the system. Youngsters, substance abusers and non-abusers alike often verbalize feelings of being picked on, singled out and feeling powerless. To move too quickly with the adolescent group to a consideration of communication skills is tempting, but the group needs time to ventilate and surface their feelings if they are to rediscover their stake in the system.

Conclusion

The Archdiocese Drug Abuse Prevention Program has trained its professional staff in the implementation of group services employing the Mutual Aid Model because it has particular relevance for substance-abuse intervention in a school setting. As previously stated, research has shown time and again the high degree of alienation among substance users. This Model places a high stake on the interaction of client and environment as a focus of the work and can result in an amelioration of some of the stress and isolation that leads to further substance abuse. Moreover, through its emphasis on peer involvement, the model takes advantage of a dynamic in adolescence that can support or preclude an individual's involvement with drugs.

Internal study of the use of the Mutual Aid model in the school setting shows promise (Gallagher, 1983). Counselors and School Personnel report increased adaptive coping among student participants. There is observed a diversity of coping style available to the students that was not evidenced prior to group involvement when the students' interactions in school were characterized largely by isolation and/or acting out. Finally, the majority of student participants begin to go through a decision making process in the group that often results in a limited, more controlled use of substances, and in many cases abstinence.

NOTES

1. From 1978 until his death, Dr. William Schwartz in the capacity of consultant devoted his time and energy assisting the ADAPP staff develop group services in schools throughout the New York Archdiocese. It is with a deep sense of gratitude to him that this paper is written describing some aspects of that work.

2. The names of the members and some of the details of the discussions have been changed to protect the confidentiality of group members. The process excerpts included in this paper were submitted as part of the agency records of service by various staff Social Workers.

REFERENCES

Gallagher, K. Improving coping in an adolescent population. (Doctoral Dissertation, Ferkauf Graduate School, Yeshiva University, 1983). *Dissertation Abstracts International.*

Halikas, J.A., Rimmer, J.D. Predictors of multiple drug abuse. *Archives of General Psychiatry,* 1974, *31*, 414-418.

Jessor, R., Jessor, S.L., Finney, J. A social psychology of marijuana use: longitudinal studies of high school and college youth. *Journal of Social Issues,* 1973, *26*(1), 1-15.

Kandel, D. Inter-and intragenerational influences on adolescent marijuana use. *Journal of Social Issues,* 1974, *30*(2), 107-135.

Kandel, D., Treiman, D., Faust, R., Single, E. Adolescent involvement in legal and illegal drug use: a multiple classification analysis. *Social Focus,* 1976, *55*(2), 438-457.

McCorry, F.A. An investigation into related personality variables among adolescents in differential patterns of marijuana use, alcohol use, and other drug use (Doctoral Dissertation, St. John's University, 1982). *Dissertation Abstracts International.*

Schwartz, W. The social worker in the group. In *New Perspectives on Services to Groups: Theory, Organization and Practice,* New York: National Association of Social Workers, 1961, 7-34.

Schwartz, W. On the use of groups in social work practice. In W. Schwartz and S. Zalba (Eds.), *The Practice of Group Work.* New York: Columbia University Press, 1971, 3-24.

Schwartz, N. Social group work: the interactionist approach. In J. Turner (Ed.), *Encyclopedia of Social Work,* Vol. II. New York: National Association of Social Workers, 1971.

Shulman, L. The *Skills of Helping Individuals and Groups.* Itasca, Illinois: F.E. Peacock Publishers, 1979.

Smith, G., Fogg, C. Psychological antecedents of teenage drug use. In R.G. Simmons (Ed.), *Research in Community and Mental Health,* Vol. I. JAI Press, 1979.

Steffenhagen, R.A., Polich, J.M., Lash, S. Alienation, delinquency, and patterns of drug use. *International Journal of Social Psychiatry,* 1978, *24*(2), 125-137.

Call for Papers

The Editors of *Social Work with Groups* announce a special issue for Volume 10, No. 3, Fall 1987.

EDUCATING SOCIAL WORKERS FOR WORK WITH GROUPS

Manuscripts addressing any of the following topics will now be received:

— Selecting knowledge and theory to inform group practice
— Dialectics of theory building: mainstream and diverse models
— Group Work's contribution to a comprehensive approach to human behavior
— Organizing principles for developing the group work curriculum: foundation and advanced
— Teaching historical, philosophical and value issues
— Research component in group work curriculum
— Cultural and diversity issues in group work
— Teaching the creative skills of activity
— The classroom as a group: experiential learning
— Field experience to support the learning of group work skills
— Supervision of group work and group methods in supervision

Deadline: July 30, 1986
Send to: Dr. Catherine P. Papell
Dr. Beulah Rothman
Co-Editors
Social Work with Groups
Adelphi University School of Social Work
Garden City, New York 11530

The Editors will welcome advanced notification of your interest in preparing papers for this issue.

Teaching as a Discovery Process: Some Core Principles Derived from William Schwartz

Nancy Boyd Webb
Michael H. Phillips

In the last years before his untimely death, Bill Schwartz devoted a good deal of his energy to looking at the process of teaching. His writings on group work note that the goal of the teacher "to teach" and the goal of the student "to learn" come together naturally in the classroom. He conceptualized the classroom as a prototype of the small group which becomes a living laboratory where student and teacher work together on a joint endeavor.

Eager to share his ideas about teaching, and curious to see how other teachers experience the process, Bill Schwartz arranged when he came to Fordham as a distinguished visiting professor in 1977 to work with a group of faculty around the dynamics of teaching. The authors were a part of that Faculty Teaching Workshop which met regularly for five years, reviewing both process recordings and video tapes of classes in order to analyze the moment-to-moment realities of the classroom and the teacher's role in the educational process. The group became convinced that the dynamics of small group functioning apply to classroom interactions, regardless of the subject or content taught.

This article presents some of the principles of teaching derived from the Faculty Teaching Workshop, under Dr. Schwartz's leadership.

Since we agree with Dr. Schwartz that learning is best demonstrated in the crucible of action, we will juxtapose examples of classroom interactions with Dr. Schwartz's own theoretical writings to illustrate some selected teaching principles. Comments from former students in Dr. Schwartz's Spring 1981 Advanced Group Work classes demonstrate Dr. Schwartz's application of the principles in his own teaching.

The five core principles we have chosen to present are not a com-

© 1986 by The Haworth Press, Inc. All rights reserved.

prehensive list, but they represent pivotal tenets that Dr. Schwartz stressed in his work with the Faculty Workshop. These core principles are:

1. Teaching and learning is a discovery process.
2. There is a need for structure within which learning takes place.
3. The teacher must model the risk-taking expected of students.
4. The teacher must forge a linkage between intellectual content and feelings.
5. The emphasis of the class must be on "the work."

It is important to realize that the above principles are not discrete. They flow together in the good group or the good class, and it usually will not be clear where one begins and another ends.

Learning as a Discovery Process

Dr. Schwartz believed that change, whether within a group or in the classroom, involves a discovery process. In the classroom the role of the teacher is that of an expert guide in what he called the common search for meanings. As he stated in a paper:

> If the learning process is seen as a quest, and the class as a party of searchers, the teacher will lay out devices and stratagems for putting this idea into action. The emphasis will be on where and how to dig, what questions to pursue, and how to use both their private work and their classroom processes to pursue them. ("Education in the Classroom": 244)

In order to create a process of discovery in the class, the teacher needs to make the topic under study alive for the students. It is not enough to define the subject; students must struggle with it to make it their own. This requires an atmosphere of inquiry in which students do not merely intellectualize about issues but grapple with their here-and-now reality. A description of a first year research methods class discussing validity highlights the concept.

> The instructor began by reminding the class about what had been covered in the last class. We built on this by defining validity and posing the question of how to test the validity of the scale we worked on the previous week. Class members

> started defining in intellectual terms how to do that. The instructor asked for specificity. One student, ''Betty'' suggested categorizing people by using the scale and measuring ''type'' against outside criteria. The instructor asked Betty to ''develop that.'' The following exchange ensured:
>
> ''I'm scared.''
> ''What about?''
> ''I'm not sure of what I'm doing.''
> ''None of us ever are when we try new things,
> but we find out things that way.''
>
> Betty then developed the idea. Another student jumped in and rephrased her statement. I asked Betty whether that is what she meant. Betty said, ''It's O.K.''
>
> I said, ''No, it's not just O.K. Is that what you were talking about?''
>
> Discussion followed between students about the degree to which outside criteria must be selected on the basis of theory. This was questioned in terms of the degree to which theory will always be culture bound. I asked for a specific example of how this idea could apply to the self-esteem scale we were developing. The class struggled together and finally described face validity, concurrent validity, predictive validity, and construct validity. After they described and defined these different approaches, the instructor labelled them for the students.

In this example the professor kept the class focussed on the work by demanding that work be in real-world terms, not intellectualization, and by giving support to the students in their effort. The professor also took responsibility to provide the labels for the insights the students evolved. This process of discovery is not the Socratic method of teaching in which professors through their questioning lead students to the ''truth.'' The Socratic method does not really involve the students in the struggle for knowledge.

Students often resist the discovery process as artificial since the professor presumably knows. Their resistance may take many forms. Students may passively wait for the professor to elaborate or merely review the content of the reading. For example, in a class the teacher described a situation in which a group of youth were resisting the group leader by having individual conversations and not relating to the efforts of the leader to get the group together. The professor then asked what the worker should have done. The students responded by asking a series of questions. "How old were the kids?" "What sort of setting was it?" "Were they required to attend?" etc. The professor gave more and more information. The class ended before there was time to confront the work.

This common occurrence must be stopped by the professor who must point out the class's resistance. The class cannot deal with the meaning of the material as long as the students' energies are focussed on getting from the professor more and more information. They must go out on an limb.

The Need for Structure

The above examples also suggest the need for the professor to set a structure within which the work takes place. Without that structure students' energies will be focussed not on the discovery process but on trying to figure out the role of the professor in the class. Dr. Schwartz believed the professor must define the parameters of the work. An example from a group work class conducted by Dr. Schwartz demonstrates how this might be done. Dr. Schwartz began the class by saying:

> "As you know, we are moving to the area of helping the group as a collective. In presentation, our main focus is on the problem of the collective and how we help people together relate to and resolve some of the issues that arise among them. The more we look at examples the smarter we will get about some of the group work skills which we need to call into play. So let's move to presentations."

The professor must set the context for the work and also point out that learning is a mutual process. Freedom to search, Dr. Schwartz used to say, can only exist within a structure. This structure provides the freedom to think independently and test thoughts in the context of other group members. The mutual aid group harnesses individual energies to the task at hand. The structure need not be oppressive to be there. As Schwartz described it:

> The need for more freedom in the classroom is not solved by the elimination of structure. In fact, and especially in the early stages of work, teacher passivity, or indecisiveness, or "per-

> missiveness,'' will engender weakness rather than strength, dependency rather than freedom. As the students sit there—uncertain, docile, unconnected to one another—they begin by needing someone who can provide an energy, force, and direction that they cannot yet muster for themselves. They are, and feel themselves to be, within the teacher's power; and they look to the teacher to offer them meaningful work, an interesting time, and a reasonable chance to learn. The teacher who is to be a guide had better look as if he knows where he is going. (''Education in the Classroom'': 244)

The need for structure does not end with the setting of the context for the class. The professor needs to guide the process, not only to bring the students together but also to keep the class focussed on the work. Thus, with a student presentation the professor must help the students probe the underlying meaning of the presenter's work. In this process the professor can be active when the group is active. When students are inactive, the professor should call attention to their inactivity rather than filling the silence with a lecture. He or she must ask, ''What is going on here?; Why is no one saying anything?'' Similarly, the presenter must be helped to identify the purpose of the presentation. As Dr. Schwartz realized, structure arises out of the demand for specificity. ''The hardest students to work with,'' he used to say, ''were the students who intellectualize because they deal with abstraction rather than concrete examples.''

As he said in ''Education in the Classroom,''

> Where the students begin to wax vague and abstracted, the teacher reaches for the specifics that will bring them back to the problems at hand. (''Education in the Classroom'': 248)

An example occurred in a class in which a student reported her problems terminating with a client who was dealing with mourning the death of her husband and with her accompanying problems of loneliness. The student indicated that she had planned to discuss termination with the client but had never been able to get to it. After several minutes of process, the professor asked:

> ''What's the purpose of your visit?'' The student responded that she didn't know if the agency had any specific goals for

> the client but that they assign the client a student each year for "support." When pressed the student stated she was trying to put the client "in touch with her own strengths."
>
> The class was silent during the exchange. The dilemma was to engage the class, so the professor asked, "Why is everyone so quiet?"
>
> One student said, "Because we are depressed," and then all laughed.
>
> "Why?" the professor responded.
>
> "Her situation makes you feel so helpless," they answered.
>
> At that point the professor could put them to work on "What could you as a social worker offer her?" and "What do you think you would want from a social worker if *you* were the client?"
>
> The ensuing discussion put students in touch with the pain they felt. One student noted that to talk about the pain of termination might have helped the client.
>
> The presenter said that talking about pain was regressive. She needed to see her strength.
>
> A re-analysis of the interview by the presenter and the class, however, showed that the presenter had been struggling with what leaving meant to *her*. She felt too close to the client to separate. With this admission the class was able to focus on what the client was saying and what her needs were.

It was through the analysis of the experience of "the moment" that the learning took place. The professor must keep up the demand by asking:

—What is the focus of the work the student does with a client?
—How does he or she read the situation?
—What are they going to do?

Out of a focus on specifics the structure of the work emerges. Discussions must be highlighted. They must not be allowed to "write a composition" to use Schwartz's words. "Tell them what they are doing; they appear to be working while not working." Demand that ''insights'' be translated into actions. Ask them to tell us how *they* would do it when they begin to criticize a presenter's intervention.

Dr. Schwartz believed that classroom teaching involves guiding students on a discovery process in which they take responsibility for their own learning. That process, however, is not totally a ''do your own thing'' process but exists within a structure created by the teacher. Structuring the class includes the following:

—Setting forth the purpose of the class
—Looking at the moment-to-moment reality
—Paying attention to feelings
—Refusal to accept abstraction and non-committal answers
—Checking back to verify understandings and communications
—Labeling what occurs

The Teacher as a Model

Just as Dr. Schwartz expected his students to put their work on the line, he was willing to expose his own work to scrutiny. This resulted in an intense involvement in the teaching/learning process on the part of both instructor and students. Dr. Schwartz did not refrain from expressing his honest opinions and thoughts about his students' work. They knew he would give them direct feedback. While this made him vulnerable to their anger at times, it also gave them an example of risking which they could use as a model in their own practice. In ''Education in the Classroom'' Dr. Schwartz stated:

> As for the students themselves, who from their vantage point know a great deal about the state of the art, there is great respect for those teachers who put their own work on the line. (''Education in the Classroom'': 251)

Dr. Schwartz's usual method of teaching involved case oriented discussions of students' process records. The students and teacher worked together to understand the meaning of the record. A tape of one of Dr. Schwartz's classes illustrated an interaction with a presenter whose record dealt with beginning a school-based group with children whose parents had been recently divorced. The student stated that she was not pleased with the level of involvement of the group—''it felt half-hearted.'' Dr. Schwartz asked the presenter the purpose of the group and then tried to involve the class in helping the presenter realize that just convening youngsters with similar life experiences was not enough. The purpose of the group had to be very explicitly stated. A student from that class commented later about Dr. Schwartz method of work:

> He did not tolerate boredom and stupidity, but he was generous in helping people work through something that was a little foolish. He didn't just pass judgement on it. He would help us look at it another way and work on it and that's kind of rare. Not just to have an opinion, but to help someone else see your feeling and work on it. He did his work with us the way he asked us to work and that takes a lot of courage.

The teacher serves as a model for students, whether for good or bad. The teacher who is consciously aware of this tries to model behavior which the students can adapt to their own practice. Thus, in reaching for negatives or conflicting points of view, the teacher conveys tolerance and respect for differences in the classroom. In dealing with the "difficult," "problematic," or "fragile" student it is often helpful for the teacher to admit to the student and class that he or she is having difficulty following the student's train of thought. This honesty on the teacher's part permits the group to also share and grapple with the difficulty and to choose whether and how to assist the problematic student toward clearer communication.

In an Advanced Practice class one student stood out as "difficult;" her comments very often were tangential to the subject and were presented in the form of convoluted "mini-lectures" which resulted in turning everyone off, including the instructor. As the semester progressed, the teacher dealt with this situation by avoiding the student's raised hand as much as possible, thus trying to limit her participation. On the occasions when the student delivered one of her "orations," the instructor handled this by either changing the subject of making a minimal comment which tended to cut off, rather than open discussion.

The instructor, who was very aware of trying to limit the student's participation, was not at all in touch with the underlying message her behavior conveyed to the class. Review of video tapes of the class in the Faculty Teaching Workshop prompted discussion of the role of the instructor as a model in dealing with the "problematic" student.

The workshop concluded that rather than avoid participation by the difficult student, the instructor has the alternative of letting the class deal with the ''deviant'' member. The instructor could effectively involve the class by saying (after a garbled comment by the problematic student), ''I'm not sure I followed that; can any of the rest of you help clarify what Mary said?'' This approach gives direct feedback to the student and permits the group of student-peers to work toward the goal of shared understanding.

An approach such as this may feel quite risky to the instructor, who may worry about whether the class is capable of dealing with the situation. Despite the risk, the potential advantage of peer mutual aid overrides the ''safer'' strategy of nonreinforcement, which inevitably conveys the negative message to the class that ''if you can't understand, or don't like, a group member, just ignore him or her!''

Linking Intellectual Content and Feelings

Another basic principle emphasized by Dr. Schwartz in his classes and in the Faculty Workshop is the obligation of the teacher to forge the linkage between head and heart, or, the intellectual content and feelings. Dr. Schwartz said:

> Feeling and knowing can no longer be polarized, but become part of the same search for meanings. (''Education in the Classroom'': 243)

In the Faculty Workshop Dr. Schwartz admonished, ''You have to get the group off its head and into its gut.'' His students remembered this principle in terms of another frequent expression of Dr. Schwartz: ''Jump in the barrel, reach for feelings.''

Asking for examples can effectively counteract intellectualization and abstraction. One class presentation involved a student's work with a group of schizophrenic in-patients who were anticipating weekend home visits with their parents. The student presenter had become uncomfortable as one patient revealed some of his fears; she (presenter) then launched into a speech about how hard it is to return home, and to interact, with one's parents. The tone of the comments resulted in a distancing effect among the patient group. Dr. Schwartz responded as follows:

> The air is electric, and you give a sermon! Is this what social work is about? The client reveals, and you conceal!''

Dr. Schwartz insisted on work invested with passion, energy and love. A student said:

> He was whole-hearted, he didn't just bring part of himself. In the classroom he would make a comment like, "How do you feel?" He would say, "You're acting like a social worker; now bring your whole feelings into the class. How do *you* feel right now? Put yourself in that person's position that you are talking to." He had a way of reaching in. That was his real special quality.

The integration of the intellectual component and the emotional was very evident in Dr. Schwartz's discussing of work during termination.

> The ending should have substance as well as feeling: where the content is stressed and the feeling repressed, there is apt to be a kind of mechanical recital of what the members "learned in school;" and where the reverse is true, there is an orgy of expressiveness, equally evasive of the total reality. The valued outcome is that the ending be not a moratorium of the work but a significant episode in it. ("Between Client and System": 194)

Emphasis on "The Work"

Dr. Schwartz viewed the teaching role as one which demanded a considerable investment of work, from both the teacher and the students. In "On the Use of Groups in Social Work Practice", Dr. Schwartz elaborated on his concept of the *demand for work.* The quotation which follows refers to the social worker's role with the client, which we believe is equally applicable to the instructor's role with students. Schwartz said:

> The worker represents what might be called the *demand for work,* in which role he tries to enforce not only the substantive aspects of the contract—what we are here for—but the conditions of work as well. This demand is, in fact, the only one the worker makes—not for certain preconceived results, or approved attitudes, or learned behaviors, but for the work itself. That is, he is continually challenging the client to address

> himself resolutely and with energy to what he came to do; and he is also, at the same time, trying to mobilize his agency to clarify what it has to offer, and to offer it wholeheartedly. (''On the Use of Groups in Social Work Practice'':11)

In ''Education in the Classroom'' Dr. Schwartz elaborates further regarding ''the work'' as this applies to classroom interactions:

> The business is more serious than they (students) had bargained for: not simply because of the amount of reading and studying—many enjoy that and are good at it—but the ''push, push, dig, dig,'' the demand that they tie their feelings to their ideas, the intensive search for real meanings, the classroom interaction with others who question and disagree, and the active participation of the teacher, who also has strongly held views. (''Education in the Classroom'': 246)

The examples of classroom interactions presented in this article, whether from Dr. Schwartz's own classes or from the classes of members of the Faculty Teaching Workshop, all emphasize the *work* focus. Something must happen in the classroom which makes the teaching/learning experience alive with meaning for students and instructor alike. It is not merely the taking of notes and completing of the required readings. It involves an intense relationship with the material which combines the intellectual and the emotional spheres. The ''demand for work,'' taken for granted by many academicians, reaches a new dimension for those who understand this expectaion in Dr. Schwartz's terms. The discovery process which comprises good teaching, and which results in exciting learning, is hard but rewarding work for both the instructor and the students.

A quote from a student from Dr. Schwartz's last Advanced Group Work class testifies compellingly the impact of William Schwartz as a master teacher:

> I think of last year as a journey for me. He taught me so much about myself not only as a professional but as a person. I think what I learned the most is to put my work out in front of the group. Not to be afraid to be criticized. That was very frightening for me. He was the one who encouraged me the most to do that and he challenged us. He made us dig deep in ourselves, to grow not only as professionals, but as people.

We who worked with Dr. Schwartz on the dynamics of teaching feel the same sense of urgency to live in the classroom the principles he helped us understand.

REFERENCES

Schwartz, W., Toward a Strategy of Group Work Practice, *Social Service Review,* September 1962, 36:3, 268-279.

Schwartz, W., On the Use of Groups in Social Work Practice, in *The Practice of Group Work,* William Schwartz & Serapio R. Zalba (eds.) New York: Columbia University Press, 1971, 3-24.

Schwartz, W., Between Client and System: The Mediating Function, in *Theories of Social Work with Groups,* Robert W. Roberts & Helen Northen (eds.) New York: Columbia University Press, 1976, 171-197.

Schwartz, W., Education in the Classroom, *Journal of Higher Education,* 1980, 51:3, 235-254.

The Log: A Creative and Powerful Teaching Tool in Social Work Education

Rhonda Ginsberg

The log requires students to struggle in an effort to bridge the gaps between theory, social work practice, and personal experience. Through the process of writing and committing ideas to paper, the log encourages intellectual risking and emotional investment. This article examines the author's experience with the log as a graduate student in William Schwartz's social group work class and illustrates Schwartz's philosophy of teaching.

Purpose of the Log

The log is a notebook in which students enter summaries of social work readings, along with their reactions. Typical entries might be addressed to the following questions: Why did the student agree or not with the author? How did the viewpoint described in the article compare with that expressed in other readings? Does the material "ring true" in terms of the student's own life experience? How specifically can the concepts be applied to work in the field? Can the ideas be connected with the discussions in the classroom?, etc.

The purpose of the log is to offer students a place to reflect on new academic material, tying it together with their own previous knowledge and experience in a way that makes the information useful, alive, and meaningful. Students use the log to *learn*—to think "out loud", to bounce around new ideas, and to jot down even only partly formulated thoughts. If this process is taken seriously and done with conviction, the log will become a very rich and important document.

In effect then, the log is a written recording of the learning pro-

© 1986 by The Haworth Press, Inc. All rights reserved.

cess—a process that includes (1) the reading of articles, (2) the integration of this material with previous personal knowledge and experience, and (3) the application of it all to concurrent work with groups. This concept of integrating "knowing", "feeling", and "doing" within the learning process is basic to Schwartz's philosophy.[1]

In using the log, the student needs to be encouraged and taught not to polarize the different parts of the learning process. For example, by focusing only on "feeling," one may confuse the log for a personal journal. While in a personal journal the mere expression of feelings may be adequate, in the log such an "indulgence" of feelings will not suffice. While the log is to include feelings and personal reactions (and would, in fact, be incomplete otherwise), it is only to include these as they relate to the task of learning social work skills. In other words, feelings in the log are viewed as a means rather than an end in and of themselves. Similarly, if one concentrates on "knowing," the log may begin to resemble a series of academic book reports in which the individual makes no investment in the learning process beyond an intellectual exercise. Moreover, if "feeling" and "knowing" are estranged from "doing," then the full purpose of the log will not be realized. When at one point I began to veer from this direction in my log, Schwartz was able to offer support while simultaneously refocusing me, writing:

> At this point, what I'm most curious about is how you're translating your growing sophistication and knowledge into social work skills. I'd like to look further with you into some of the *moments* in which you feel you are—and aren't—producing the skilled response the kids need . . . The "piece of process" you included in your log (2/2) was expressive and beautifully written, but there was almost nothing about what you *did* in relation to any of the host of stimuli with which you were bombarded. The *reflection* in your writing—throughout your log—is sensitive, lovely, sometimes profound—but how specifically, do you turn these ideas and feelings into action? (3/7/78)

The Log as a Vehicle for the Creative Process

Active struggle is required to develop the connection between the different entities of "knowing", "feeling", and "doing" in order to make the learning process complete.[2] Interestingly, the concept of struggle is also identified as basic to the creative process. Theorists describe the phenomenon of "creative stress," a mix of data, observations, and emotions which contradict each other and do not blend with existing modes of thought.[3] Such stress is viewed as a necessary variable to set the creative process in motion. However, the conception of an idea is viewed by one theorist as only the first stage of the creative process. The second stage, the one in which the idea is actually carried out, is then characterizied by discipline, stubbornness, patience, training, practice, and just plain hard work.[4]

The learning process encouraged by the log parallels the creative process. The log provides the *structure* to allow students to search for answers rather than simply supplying the answers alone. The log demands an active, creative process of learning as opposed to a passive one. Students learn by questioning, reflecting, tearing apart, and recreating—not by memorizing. Consequently, the log requires a great deal of time and work, but simultaneously offers an opportunity for immense gratification.

The following is an example of one of those cherished moments in the log (though one may not be sure of it at the time) when the struggle to clarify one's thoughts allows one to discover an answer that is the result of truly applying the concepts one has been taught. This entry was in response to a log assignment by Schwartz to apply a theoretical group work model to a specific group.

> I selected a model of group stages of development conceptualized by Bennis and Shephard. As I read B. & S.'s article, I tried to think of ways in which to apply their concepts to any groups with which I am familiar (i.e.—our group class, my group of 4th grade boys, the Jungian group), and I had a really tough time applying their theory in any "holistic" way—I was really only able to pick out "bits and pieces" which I could exemplify with the groups I knew about. Thus, my first question here is *can* B. & S.'s concepts be applied to groups whose tasks differ from those of the groups on which B. & S. base their theory? (B. & S. write on p.66: "This theory is based for the most part on observations made over a 5 year period of teaching graduate students 'group dynamics.' The main function of the seminar as it was set forth by the instructors was to improve the internal communication system of the group, hence a self-study group.")

> In answer to this question, I have several thoughts.
>
> First, maybe we *can* generalize B. & S.'s ideas to other groups, but perhaps my problem in doing so is due to the *newness* of the groups I've got in mind. Maybe because these groups are only in the very beginning stages of B. & S.'s developmental theory, I am lacking in enough information to make an accurate assessment of the applicability of B. & S.'s *entire* theory of development which goes from the beginning of groups to the end.
>
> On second thought though, maybe we *can't* apply B. & S.'s theory because their groups are "problem-ridden" from the *start* and so "doomed" to follow the path that B. & S. describe, a path that is *not* a necessary one for all groups. How are B. & S.'s groups "problem-ridden"? It seems to me that the purpose of B. & S.'s groups is quite circular and a bit unclear. (This lack of clarity, however, could indeed be due to the fact that the purpose is only mentioned and described briefly in a footnote in the article.) However, from the short description of group purpose in the article, it sounds like B. & S.'s groups were a study of group "process", without any regard for group "content". In other words, it sounds like B. & S. set up classes in "group dynamics" in which they learned by studying themselves as a group and by attempting to "improve the internal communication system of the group"; yet just *what* they were communicating about seems to have been left out—*That,* I would guess, could create a lot of problems and confusion . . .
>
> Well, now that I've clarified the possible reasons why I had trouble applying B. & S.'s thoughts to the groups with which I am familiar, let me try to apply their theory anyway as best I can. (11/24/77)[5]

Schwartz supported both my viewpoint and my struggle, writing:

> Your hunch about the B. & S., framework—that it's "tied up with this particular type of group"—is absolutely correct. My own idea is that Bennis & Shepard *created,* by their kind of leadership, a whole lot of problems the group then had to solve. But, in an interesting way, there was a lot that happened that turned out to be common to *many* kinds of groups. (As it turned out, you figured a lot of this out for yourself.)

It should be noted that the creative thinking process encouraged by the log can also be viewed as educative in and of itself, beyond the actual content that the log explores. Teaching students to be creative helps them to better cope, be it in a quickly changing world or a bureaucratic system. It also arms them with the ability to think for themselves, hopefully making them more confident individuals as well.

In working on the log, one may become so absorbed that hours pass by in a flash and one's surroundings are forgotten. Yet in spite of the concentration and hard work, one emerges feeling energized and enriched. In the literature on creativity, theorists refer to this aspect of the creative process as "the loss of self".[6] I tried to describe this feeling in my final note to Schwartz at the end of the semester, writing, "It's kind of hard to end this log—it's been so meaningful for me, almost a 'place' that was rich and real that I could escape to and step inside . . ." (4/26/78)

I believe that the "place" to which I was referring was actually the place inside of me (and inside all of us) where emotions, intuition, gut feelings, and maybe even innate wisdom all originate. People refer to it differently, calling it one's "gut", "heart", "creative life force", "id", "unconscious", etc.

For me, "the loss of self" via the creative process was one of the most important aspects of the log. The log provided me with a ladder into the richness of the unconscious—a safe means to climb down and back out again, dipping into this rich and powerful material and raising it up to a conscious level to incorporate it with both academic and practice issues. To put it differently, it allowed me "to reach into the gut" or "to speak from the heart."[7]

The Log as a Dialogue

The log may be thought of as a dialogue in a variety of ways—as a dialogue within oneself, a cross-dialogue between oneself and the various authors of the readings, and a dialogue (or role-play of sorts) between oneself and one's clients. However, the log may be viewed as a dialogue in still one more way: the log can serve to provide a rich meeting ground for dialogue with a knowledgeable and caring teacher.

After being immersed in only my own thoughts via the log, I welcomed the opportunity to gain some perspective on my work via the response of another person. Here one may draw a parallel between the log and a social work group. In both cases, there is an almost pressing need to find out one is not alone by seeking an exchange outside oneself, searching for both one's commonality and uniqueness.

In order for a student to talk freely enough to risk, flounder, open up, and grow it is critical for the teacher to create a safe and protected environment that enables such a process to occur. How specifically can this be done?

To begin with, much as a worker does with clients, a teacher must be able to demonstrate to students caring, acceptance, and the willingness to share the pain of the struggle to learn. This may be conveyed by one's tone of voice, one's energy for the work, one's feedback in the log, etc. To do this, the teacher must be able to bridge the gap between the role of professor and him or herself as a human being. If the teacher can risk being "real"—not hiding behind a role, glossing over conflict, or backing away from genuine feelings—then students can begin to do the same. The goal is the gradual development of trust between student and teacher.

These concepts are reflected in Schwartz's comments in the log, a powerful combination of poetic metaphors, honed insights, honest questions, gut reactions, and genuine praise. His responses were so vivid and gratifying that I still remember many of his words years later. In one instance, his response came alive with a warm touch of humor when he wrote: "There's so much great stuff in your log that my comments feel like a drop of water in the ocean. However, just a couple . . ."

As with social group work, when the *purpose* of the classwork is clear, students are more able to relax and get on with the task of learning. Knowing that the teacher will "stick to the work", students can be open with no fear of personal invasion by being "caseworked" or "psychoanalyzed."

Giving students permission to struggle and to not always have neat answers, also allows for a more open dialogue. In addition, if students know that their views will be respected and received in a non-judgmental fashion, they can more freely express their thoughts. However, at the same time it should be emphasized that this does not preclude the role of the teacher to make a "demand for work". In truth, one of the ways a teacher expresses caring is by making this demand.

As a focus for dialogue and interaction between teacher and student, the log also becomes one of the potential "battlegrounds" for the struggle with authority. One of the very purposes of the log is to encourage students to question, challenge, and struggle; thus issues associated with the teacher as an authority figure emerge more openly than they might in another type of setting. Hence, within my group work class, some students resisted Schwartz regarding the freedom of the log assignment (i.e.—choice of readings, no clear "right" answers for comments on readings, etc.). They demanded an answer to the questions, "But what are we *supposed* to do? What do *you want*?" Schwartz of course didn't budge, demanding that they "work" and "risk"—and the fight was on. Though I was certainly not immune to a desire for the teacher's approval, some part of me understood Bill's challenge; I was hungry for the chance to be set free to gobble up all the material I'd been curious about until then, but lacked the structure to pursue solely on my own.

Finally, the log as a dialogue can serve still one more absolutely critical purpose. At the end of the term I wrote to Schwartz:

> Thanks for all your help this year and for offering me the chance to *share* all these thoughts. You've given me a great deal of confidence with regard to the value of my own ideas and I've carried it over elsewhere as well; your comments were always so real and warm that I was usually "high" for days afterwards! I'm gonna miss you, but I really feel as if you've given me something that's now a part of me . . . (4/26/78)

Hence, Schwartz's feedback enabled me to develop a real *faith* in the value of my own ideas, as well as a sharper sense of my own unique qualities and worth. That perhaps, next to the log itself, was the most important gift he gave me.

Suggestions for the Use of the Log

For students and teachers who plan to utilize the log, the following section contains specific "nitty-gritty" suggestions culled from own experience with the log, as well as course procedures used by Schwartz. The ideas offered here are best applied with flexibility to accommodate individual preferences.

Style of Entries: Reactions in the log should be one's own as opposed to thoughts to please or impress the teacher. Wording should be clear rather than bogged down in lofty, complicated, and empty jargon. It helps to keep a sense of humor and to maintain one's natural curiosity. The point to bear in mind is that the learning must be kept meaningful for oneself.

Schwartz reinforced these concepts in his response to my first log entries, encouraging me to ''dare'' to shape my own style in the log. He wrote:

> You use your log very well—your reading is diversified, and your reactions are original and close to your own experience. I enjoyed your comments about the group experience and your relation to it—your penetrating comment about the ''phony intimacy'', and you handled the Wheelis piece quite well. I'm looking forward to seeing more of your work, as you loosen up some more and build more faith in your own ideas—Nice Start—(9/78).

As I became comfortable with the log, I rapidly discovered that I was able to put my thoughts on paper in an organized flow, as they would have come to me in conversation. This, in combination with the fact that there simply was not time enough to copy over pages of notes, helped me to realize (much to my surprise) that I could write well the first time without rewrites. The log not only allowed me to make this discovery, but to practice and develop it as well. Such a skill has since proven important to me professionally in terms of both confidence and efficiency.

This view of the log as an extended conversation is highlighted briefly in my own log. With regard to a passage concerning my struggles with a group of latency-aged boys, I quipped: ''Sheesh, in re-reading this it sounds more like a letter to Dear Abby!''

Bibliographic References: A bibliographic reference for each article that is read should appear at the top of the entry page (author, title, publisher, page, etc.). In this way, one can easily refer back to the article if necessary at some future point.

Direct Quotes: Direct quotes from the article, with the page number recorded in the notebook margin, are a useful and easy way to make note of important concepts. Sometimes, however, isolated quotes do not fully convey an idea or theme, and in such instances a brief summary in one's own words may be helpful. A good concept to bear in mind here is to take notes as if writing a term paper—use the notes as a way of remembering and learning what was said to avoid the need to go back to the original source.

Re-reading an article in order to copy down quotes or summarize points for the log also forces one to further think through the material and truly understand it. In so doing, the student may become cognizant of a previously unforeseen discrepancy in thought and be "forced" to unravel the contradictions.

Subheadings: One should try to organize thoughts while writing, starting a new paragraph with each new idea. It may be helpful to use subheadings to elucidate themes, inserting them as one goes along or adding them in afterwards in the margin.

Spacing: Space entries to facilitate easier reading and re-reading, leaving blank lines between sections. It helps make the material feel less overwhelming, especially after scribbling away deep in thought only to find oneself with pages full of ideas.

Color and Personalized Working Tools: For this writer, color is an important concept in general, and, hence, it somewhat unwittingly became a part of the log. Colored pens often supplied that little extra needed push to get started on schoolwork. Colored inks also made the log itself more visually appealing, further inspiring looking through and re-reading. Color may also be used for the more practical purpose of coding with regard to topics, ideas, articles, etc. Students should become more cognizant of creative "methods" that facilitate their work, applying them to the log where possible.

Conclusion

Schwartz suggests that the teacher provide a course outline which defines the course topics or "Areas of Investigation." Readings for the log are to be done in conjunction with these "areas," as they are sequentially addressed in class. The outline should include a large bibliography from which students may select particular readings which most interest them. A demand for extensive reading should be made by the teacher.[8]

Schwartz utilized the log in lieu of exams. He collected and read the logs several times a semester returning them not with grades, but with helpful comments and reactions. Students were always free to request that he look at their log at any point to ask questions, get feedback, and/or arrange an individual conference.

Schwartz gave no advance notice of collection dates in order to encourage students to work regularly (as opposed to trying to meet a deadline at the last minute). The underlying concept here was that it is impossible to "cram" a log assignment in the way that one can cram for a test. Time is a necessary, creative element of the log, allowing for reflection and the mulling over of new ideas.

Throughout the year, students struggled with Schwartz's demands for extensive and creative work, the freedom of the log assignment, and the requirement that they take responsibility for their own learning. However, at the same time they grew and thrived in the atmosphere of individualization, challenge, excitement, and caring that Schwartz created.

William Schwartz was an outstanding educator. The log is an example of one of the many instruments he developed to offer students an active and gripping learning experience. However, it is important that the log be viewed in the larger context of Schwartz's social work philosophy. His ideas about teaching methods parallel his ideas about social group work: both, for example, emphasize the need for clarity of purpose to facilitate tasks, a demand for work by the leader, and emotional investment on the part of students and group members.[9] Hence, the log may be viewed as a microcosm of Schwartz's overall values and concepts and stands as still one more illustration of his contribution to the fields of education and social work practice.

NOTES

1. Alex Gitterman, ''Comparison of Educational Models and Their Influcences on Supervision'' in Florence Whiteman Kaslow (ed.), *Issues in Human Services.* San Francisco: Jossey-Bass, Inc., 1972, pp. 18-39.

2. The concept of struggle is central to Schwartz's thinking-be it within the classroom, the group, or systems work. Schwartz stressed the importance of a notion which precipitates conflict rather than avoids it. This, in part, formed the underpinnings for his view of the social worker as ''mediator.''

In the classroom, Schwartz demanded that the students ''jump in'', get down to ''the nitty-gritty,'' and stop ''bebbering'' in ''professional word salad,'' ''jargon,'' and ''global terms.'' He asked for ''goals'' as opposed to ''prayers.'' He was indeed a ''pro'' at spotting the ''dozens of ways in which they (students) try to avoid the pain of the work as well as the pain of the struggle right here in class to learn from the work.'' (William Schwartz, ''Education in the Classroom'', *Journal of Higher Education,* Ohio State University Press, Volume 51, No. 3, p. 17.)

3. Arthur Koestler, ''Regression and Integration'' in Walt Anderson (ed.), *Therapy and the Arts-Tools of Consciousness.* New York: Harper and Row, 1977, pp. 3-10.

4. Abraham Maslow, ''The Creative Attitude,'' in Walt Anderson (ed.), *Therapy and the Arts-Tools of Consciousness.* New York: Harper and Row, 1977, pp. 11-28.

5. Warren G. Bennis & Herbert A. Shepard, ''A Theory of Group Development,'' in Warren G. Bennis, Kenneth D. Benne, & Robert Chin (eds.), *The Planning of Change* (New York: Holt, Rinehart, and Winston, 1962), pp. 321-40.

6. Abraham Maslow, op cit., p. 16.

7. At a memorial service at Fordham, Derrick Carter referred to a dream he had about

Bill Schwartz, describing a vivid image of music in a frame. This brings to my mind a vision of animated notes dancing joyfully about inside a beautiful antique frame, sweet sounds pouring forth. In essence, this image provides a perfect metaphor for the relationship of the log to the creative process. Just as the frame in the dream provides a structure to preserve the kinetic music without disturbing its freshness and spirit, the log too provides a structure to preserve the beauty of the creative process, despite its somewhat abstract and elusive qualities.

8. William Schwartz, ''Education in the Classroom,'' *Journal of Higher Education.* Ohio State University Press, Volume 51, No. 3, 1980.

9. William Schwartz & Serapio R. Zalba, ''Groups in Social Work Practice'' in William Schwartz & Serapio R. Zalba (eds.), *The Practice of Group Work.* New York: Columbia University Press, 1971, pp. 3-24.

Call for Papers

For Special Issue of *Social Work with Groups*

THE CONCEPT OF COLLECTIVITY: OPERATIONALIZING THEORY

Guest Editors: Norma C. Lang[1] and Joanne Sulman

This special issue of the journal *Social Work with Groups* calls for papers focussed on practice in small social forms which are not quite group, and which may be unable to develop their potential to become full-fledged groups. These less-developed small social forms, described as *collectivities*[1], may arise because of the way in which a key variable in group life is managed, or is outside of the control of the worker and the members.

Papers are invited which:

—report on practice with a particular collectivity
—explore the inherent capability of a particular kind of collectivity for helping purposes
—examine the adaptations to the worker role when the entity cannot become a group
—apply the theory to an example from practice, and critique the practice
—extend the theory or critique the theory

Papers should conform to the requirements for manuscripts for *Social Work with Groups.*
Deadline for Submitting Papers—April 1, 1986.

Submit papers to: Dr. Norma C. Lang
Faculty of Social Work
University of Toronto
246 Bloor Street West
Toronto, Ontario, M5S 1A1

[1]Lang, N.C. Social Work Practice in Small Social Forms: Some unacknowledged Entities. In N. Goroff (ed.). *Reaping from the Field: From Practice to Principle*. Proceedings, Third Symposium on Social Work with Groups, Vol. II, Hebron, Conn.: Practitioners Press, 1983.

The Use of a Diary in Social Work Education

Yvonne Taylor Cullen

ABSTRACT. This article discusses the use of a diary in the education process with particular reference to social work. Differences between a private diary and one used for educational purposes are considered as are the student/teacher and student/student relationships, which are of central importance in the use of such a device. The problems and difficulties faced by students in using a diary as a vehicle in which to integrate reading, classroom discussion and field practice, in a subjective and scholarly manner, are examined. Issues such as confidentiality, and evaluation are discussed.

Integrating theory and practice is still one of the most central problems confronting social work. Finding ways of enabling students to become creative, adaptable persons who can critically refine what they do, in some degree of harmony with what they think and believe, is not an easy task. This applies particularly in an educational system which still tends to view students as reservoirs of knowledge or slaves to a particular set of techniques, despite the fact that educational theorists have continuously stressed that learners need to perceive the relationship of knowledge and experience to themselves to be touched by them. As long ago as 1897, Dewey wrote that "education must be conceived of as the continuing restructuring of experience; the process and the goal of education are one and the same thing."[1] More recently, Desiderius Orban speaking of artists, highlights the same dichotomy:

> . . . there is a great difference between a painter and an artist. The painter is a craftsman, he learns the trade how to paint pic-

This article is republished with permission from *The Journal of the Australian Association of Social Workers* 34 (Dec. 1981): 21-24. We are sad to inform you that the author has recently passed away.

The author wrote, "I wish to express my gratitude to Dr. William Schwartz, who first introduced me to the diary at Columbia University in 1969. The diary format that I consequently adapted for use in my own social work teaching was based on one originally developed by him."

© 1981 by *The Journal of the Australian Association of Social Workers.*

> tures, sometimes with great virtuosity. The craftsman is not an artist because he doesn't create a new world, he imitates the existing world. The artist's creation is based on an inborn idea which is stimulated by the outside world.[2]

Students express the need to practice as thoughtful skilled people and the following comment reflects what appears to be a widely felt unease amongst social work students.

> We can develop a cosy analysis of society and what is wrong with it, e.g. the causes of the gross unemployment of youth in this country, but knowing what is wrong hasn't given me any confidence in knowing what to do to help rectify it.[3]

Educators have attempted to find ways of bringing experience and knowledge more closely together through many avenues of experiential learning such as the use of audio visual methods, role play, simulation, etc., and one method I employ to assist students to make some sense of their material is through the use of an educational journal or diary. The aim is to provide a vehicle in which students are free to reflect, to question and search for answers, regarding the issues and conflicts that arise in their work. To this end I ask them to keep an ongoing journal in which to analyse critically and to comment on the literature experienced in the classroom, in the field practice and, in fact, in any other situation that they see as relevant to their work. The minimum requirement is that entries be made systematically and regularly and that they be focused on a majority of topics that form the basis of the relevant course, with all appropriate source material recorded. The diary can then develop as an enduring and scholarly resource for students' current and future use. It is more appropriately located in courses depending on a face-to-face or small group format.

Initially students show caution to agreeing to take on such an assignment for usually this is the first time they are being asked to incorporate their own personal impressions and experiences into their work. The following is typical of students' first reactions:

> I began this diary with some apprehension as I am not sure that I can adequately express my honest thoughts and impressions about my experiences in learning to become a 'social worker'! . . . I often have difficulty in verbally expressing

> what I feel about certain experiences so I hope that the diary may provide some insight into learning about myself. I chose to do this course on group work primarily because I know that I would have to take responsibility for my own learning rather than just sit back in a tutorial and listen to a teacher rave on about some subject.[3]

Another common student worry is expressed in the following diary entry:

> Not only am I expected to reveal to you and my fellow students what I know and think but also what I am doing in my attempts to practice social work. Since I feel very inadequate in this, the whole idea is overwhelming.[5]

The use of a scholarly diary is not new. My first experience of it was as a social work student myself when, for the first time in a long educational career, I was expected to write myself . . . to examine my own responses and try to make sense of what I was taking from my readings and practice. I, too, responded with apprehension, for like the students quoted above, I was wary of expressing my uncertain opinions even to myself, let alone to the teacher and my fellow students.[7]

In my search through the literature prior to writing this article, I found diaries and journals being used by educators from fields as diverse as English literature, the social sciences and natural sciences, who were working in a range of educational establishments from elementary schools to universities. Therapists and counsellors were also notable in their use of such a method.[7,8,9] They all had the same end in view, which was to help students, clients and, in some cases, teachers to ruminate on and question what they were reading, doing and thinking. As one writer suggested to her students: "Journals are places to create, experiment, write, jot, make mistakes and revise. They'll help you bring what is inside and outside you together in a way that makes sense."[10] With regard to Social Work education Bertha C. Reynolds, as early as 1942, in *Learning and Teaching in Social Work* refers to her use of 'working note books' as a means of enabling social work students, ". . . to break through the tight compartments in which most people keep their interests, seeing the living material of social work in relation to the price of fish, the latest popular song, a new theory of the treatment of disease, recent legislation, or whatever concerns human beings."[11]

However, with the exception of a recent article on the use of diaries with experimental groups,[12] there appeared to be little else published on the use of such a device in social work education.[13]

Subjectivity and the Educational Diary

Primarily, a diary is written for oneself and its most important function is to be a forum for the writer's uninhibited thoughts, feelings, and ideas. Anne Frank illustrated the private nature of the personal diary when she wrote:

> . . . It's an odd idea for someone like me to keep a diary; not only because I have never done so before, but because it seems to me that neither I . . . nor for that matter anyone else . . . will be interested in the unbosomings of a 13 year old school girl. Still what does it matter? I want to write, but more than that I want to bring out all kinds of things that lie buried in my heart.[14]

This does not mean that the educational diary should not contain intimate and autobiographical material, but such material is only appropriate when it has direct relevance to the students' learning. The basic difference between the purely personal diary and the educational one is that the author of the former can *choose* to show it to others whilst the educational one is *designed to be shared,* which means expecting students to risk themselves and their work both with their teacher and fellow students. This is a heavy demand to place on students and it is essential that teachers be sensitive to the students' readiness to reveal private material even when it is course related. For example, early in a social work course, a student having read *On Death and Dying* by E. Kubler-Ross,[15] wrote in her diary:

> . . . it was reassuring and encouraging to confirm that the views I had developed out of my own experience could be a tool to help others. I think there should be more community education so as to stop what someone has called the 'pornography' of death: we all know it occurs but we insist on covering it up with mystery and silence.[16]

She then gave examples of how she attempted to use emotive words such as 'dying' when talking to a terminally ill client. It was clear from this entry, i.e. 'views I had developed out of my own experience', that the student was referring to something very real in her own life. The teacher concerned chose to let it pass but towards the end of the year long course, following a class seminar on death and dying, the student again returned to the subject. She now drew on her intimate experiences related to the tragic death, from cancer, of her young husband three years previously. The following are some excerpts from her diary:

> My husband died three days before the eight weeks he was given had elapsed, he was 29 . . . my struggle with social prejudice started then—people seemed to avoid me. I now realise why but at the time I felt terribly confused and had so much violence inside me that I was always afraid of assaulting someone. . . . However, a major breakthrough occurred three weeks later . . . My mother and I were helping my aunt peel cucumbers. My aunt turned around and asked me very much matter-of-factly: 'Did J. like cucumbers?' My mother was shocked and gave my aunt a fierce look. My aunt caught the message: 'I feel we have to talk to N. about J. He was her husband, we can't go on playing ignorance, pretending nothing had happened!'' The student concludes: 'I don't usually publicize my experience, mainly because it concerns someone else, as well as me, but I have found this experience very useful in my fieldwork.[17]

Whilst the use of intimate material must be optional, subjectivity is a necessary part of the educational diary. The latter refers to the expectation that students reflect on their opinions and reactions and relate material to their experiences. To facilitate this they are asked to use the first person. This is asking them to write in a much more personal way than has usually been their wont. The following illustrates a student's first attempt to do this:

> '*20th March.* In these early weeks of the Social Work course it seemed like a good idea, today, when we decided in class to do some hard and honest thinking about what the function of social work really is in our society and why we are in it. However, now that I have begun the reading and thinking, I'm

> beginning to realise that some of my conclusions, if honest, are going to be painful for me to face. For instance, J. Galper, *(Politics of Social Services,* Prentice Hall, NJ. 1975) comments that political functions serve to encourage conformity and conservatism in both clients and workers. I think this is true for our society (Australia) as well as the U.S.A. It does seem to me that social work is little more than an instrument of social control. Indeed many of the texts unashamedly state this to be a specific function of a social worker. See for example, Pincus, A. and Minahan, A., *Social Work Practice,* N.Y. 1973, p. 15. I think it would be unrealistic for me to kid myself that whilst social work is about maintaining the status quo, I, personally, am not.[18]

The Diary as a Means of Dialogue Between Students and Teachers

The diary has the potential for promoting dialogue between students and teacher and facilitating critical thinking, which Paulo Friere points out is:

> . . . thinking which perceives reality as a process, as a transformation, rather than a static entity . . . thinking which does not separate itself from action, but constantly immerses itself in temporality without fear of the risks involved.[19]

The difficult task is only possible if the teacher is aware of, and open about, the power imbalance that is inevitable in the student/teacher relationship, even in a school committed to student centered learning. For teachers inevitably hold authority over students because of their 'expertise', supposed greater knowledge and their mandate to pass or fail students—in short, because they are official representatives of the institution that employs them. Such power imbalance will remain an insurmountable barrier to any dialogue unless a teacher is prepared to give a frank and realistic declaration of where she or he stands in this regard. This is particularly important at the beginning of a course when the teacher is such an unknown quantity to students. Thus teachers need to be prepared to talk openly about their own beliefs, feelings and experiences with students, and discuss, with them, the dimensions of their authority role. Futher, they can attempt to personalize their comments in feedback to the students in their diaries. Or even keep a diary along with the students[20] "not as a peer, but as one involved in the learning experience."[21] In fact, one writer urged "student to read and write comments in his or her (teacher's) journal when appropriate."[22] If a genuine dialogue is built up, learning gaps (and teaching gaps) are more easily identified, for such a process puts teachers in direct contact with the students' struggle to learn and makes it possible to provide more individualized guidance for them. Further, if a climate of trust is operating, students will gradually be prepared to give teachers honest feedback about the course and their teaching. One student wrote,

> I found it very helpful when you took part in the role play in class today. It relaxed the atmosphere and made me feel more equal and that you were not just the expert watching us.[23]

Yet another commented,

> I think it would be helpful if, before class ends, we could spend a short time reviewing what we have done and summing things up a bit. At present a lot of our work gets lost because we leave it too fragmented.[24]

If teachers take such entries seriously, students will then have the opportunity to contribute to, and take some responsibility for, the shaping of the course and the learning/teaching process.

Student/Student Dialogue

The use of current diary entries in the classroom can be a very fruitful way of fostering cohesion and a spirit of collective learning in the classroom. Their use also serves to diffuse some of the fantasies students have about one another's ability, as well as providing a source for them to benefit from others' study. One commented:

> I learned a lot from A's reading of his diary entry in which he openly revealed his conflicts about taking the role of a leader rather than a peer in the group for young boys he runs at his agency. It made me realise that I, too, have similar difficulties when working with people my own age, although I had never really admitted it to myself before. Moreover, our discussion with him, made me feel much more comfortable with A. and with the rest of the class for that matter.[25]

Such sharing with peers has the added advantage of breaking down the role of the teacher as the sole commentator and ever watchful evaluator, or even of the beneficient mentor. It also enables students to benefit from one another's reading and experience and gives them the opportunity to reflect on and evaluate their own and others' work in a relatively safe environment which will be a rare luxury once they are professionally employed.

Confidentiality is also an important issue when using the diary and the terms of it are best contracted with the students at the commencement of the course, so that the terms of reference are clear and accepted by both students and teachers. In my experience, the staff members teaching courses where the diary has been used have operated as a team and the students have related to them as such. Student permission has been sought for the teaching team to be free to share the diaries among themselves, if for no other reason than for teachers to learn from one another in the use of the diary. For any use outside this, the students' permission was specifically requested.

The Problem of Assessment

The thrust of the previous discussion concerns the diary as a means of focusing on the educational process. Thus for teachers to assess the diary defeats its purpose by suppressing the spirit of free inquiry and candid individual and group discussion which it is meant to promote. This does not mean that it is not given credit in a course. For instance, I expect the diary to meet the following criteria:

1. that diary entries be ongoing and regular;
2. that wide reading, at least from the course material, be critically examined and reflected on;
3. that students attempt to integrate the literature and their practice with emphasis on how they are subjectively affected by them, and
4. that students be willing to share current entries in class discussion, from time to time.

In other words, students either invest themselves in the endeavor or they don't. Carroll expressed a similar view by urging her readers not to "grade the journals except in terms of completeness, effort, growth, and creativity . . . How else can you 'mark' an extension of someone's self?''[26] After all, through the diary, students have made the process of their education visible throughout the course, both to the teacher and their fellow students. If honest feedback has been part of this, it would seem that assignments for evaluation of the course, in addition to the diary, would be superfluous. Hart made the point that term papers may be more polished but that the originality of diary entries, reflecting the students' own searchings, were of much more importance.[27] Further, Miller and Miller commented that diaries are not only individually ''unique, creative and non-plagiarizable,''[28] but that they give students continuous practice in writing and organizing the matter of the course.[29]

Keeping a diary takes time and this needs to be taken into account if students are to be given the opportunity of pursuing this more autonomous method of study. Consequently, the diary needs to be set for a specific period of time and not for more than one course at a time. Moreover, unless teachers are serious about using such a device, as a means of enabling students to be able to write in a scholarly and subjective way, and are prepared to invest the necessary time in reading and responding to them, there is little point in using them.

Some Conclusions

Teaching is a substantial part of many social workers' activities. Most are involved, as least from time to time, in student supervision and many regularly teach, part time, on social work and welfare courses. Moreover, social workers are becoming increasingly involved in interdisciplinary training programmes and workshops for groups such as volunteers who work in emergency counseling service, refuges and the like. It would seem to me that the diary may be one useful means of engaging participants in the complex and personally demanding task of making sense of such programmes by helping them to own and understand what they believe and do.

REFERENCES

1. The subject of this paper was previously sketched by the present author in a short article, entitled ''A Tool for Assessment in a Social Work Practice Course'' in *Contemporary Social Work Education,* Vol. 2, No. 1, May 1978, pp. 41-55.

2. John Dewey. ''My Pegagogic Creed'', in *Dewey on Education,* Classics in Education, No. 3, Teachers College Press, N.Y. 1967, p. 27.

3. "Desiderius Orban", an interview in *Aspect,* 5, 1-2, 1980. Sydney.

4. Student Diary, No. 1, 1980.

5, 6. Student Diary, No. 2, 1980.

7. I wish to express my gratitude to Dr. William Schwartz, who first introduced me to the diary at Columbia University in 1969. The diary format that I consequently adapted for use in my own social work teaching was based on one originally developed by him.

8. Teresa Tuzil, "Writing: A Problem Solving Process", *Social Work,* January, 1978, pp. 67-70.

9. G. Sainty, "The Diary as an Aid to the Counsellor", *The School Counsellor,* 19, March 1972, p. 293-6.

10. R. J. Riordan, & K. B. Matheny, "Dear Diary: Logs in Group Counselling". *Personal and Guidance Journal,* 50: 5, 1972, pp. 379-82.

11. Joyce Carroll, "The Written Word is not Dead", *Media and Methods,* 9.3, 1972, p. 62.

12. B. C. Reynolds, *Learning and Teaching in the Practice of Social Work,* Rinehart & Co. Inc. N.Y. 1942, p. 157.

13. Richard A. Mackey & Bernard O'Brien, "The Use of Diaries with Experiential Groups", in *Social Work with Groups,* 2:2, 1979.

14. For instance, *The Journal of Education for Social Work,* 1968-1978 inclusively, carried no relevant articles.

15. Anne Frank, *The Diary of a Young Girl,* Doubleday and Co. Inc., New York, 1952, p. 11.

16. Elizabeth Kubler-Ross. *On Death and Dying.* Tavistock Publications, London, 1970.

17, 18. Student Diary, No. 3, 1977.

19. Student Diary, No. 4, 1977.

20. Paulo Friere, *Pedagogy of the Oppressed,* Seabury Press, N.Y. 1968, p. 81.

21. For an interesting discussion of science teachers' use of a diary in teacher education courses, see E. Labinowich, "Affective-Cognitive Integration in Science Education for Facilitation of Teacher Change", *Science Education,* 60:4, 1976, pp. 513-9.

22. Carroll, "The Written Word . . ." p 62.

23. Lott Jesse. "Classroom Journals", *Social Education,* January, 1978. p. 16.

24. Student Diary, No. 5, 1979.

25. Student Diary, No. 6, 1979.

26. Student Diary, No. 7, 1980.

27. Carroll, op. cit. p 63.

28. N. I. Hart, "Using the Personal Journal in Literature Teaching", *Reading Improvement,* 9: Winter 1972, p. 89.

29. R. Miller & R. S. Miller, "The Student's Sociological Diary", *Teaching Sociology,* 4, 1, 1976.

30. Miller & Miller, "The Student's Sociological Diary".

RELATED READINGS

Other relevant references not directly quoted from in this article.

Michael Platt, "Writing Journals in Courses," *College English,* 37:4, December 1975, pp. 408-10.

Michael J. Herrick, "Diaries: Discovering the Journal." *Teaching English in a Two Year College,* 2:2, 1976, pp. 89-94.

Michael Crabbie, "Someone to tell my troubles to . . . ," *The School Counsellor,* 20: May 1973, pp. 389-91.

Tristine Rainer, *The New Diary,* Angus & Robertson, Sydney, 1980.

BOOK REVIEW

AN INTRODUCTION TO GROUP WORK PRACTICE. Ronald W. Toseland and Robert F. Rivas. *New York: Macmillan, 1984, 385 pp.*

The purpose of the book is to synthesize and integrate existing knowledge about the practice of group work with treatment and task groups, and to build a bridge between process oriented, group-centered models of practice and individual-centered, structural models of practice. In a foreword, Max Siporin leads the reader to expect an ecological systems approach that facilitates a fruitful use of psychodynamic, behavioral, and other orientations to practice. The book contains a great deal of excellent material, but it describes clearly a structural model of practice which does not utilize psychodynamic orientations to understanding people in their situations. More specifically, the model for treatment groups is essentially behavior and task-centered; for task groups, it is essentially problem-solving.

The definition of group work used by the authors is: "goal-directed activity with small groups of people aimed at meeting socio-emotional needs and accomplishing tasks. The activity is directed to individual members of a group and to the group as a whole within a system of service delivery" (p. 12). The definition encompasses both treatment and task groups. Along with a description of generic components of knowledge and skills, the differences among types of groups within each major category are compared in a thorough fashion, and attention is given to intervention in both the group and the environment in which the group functions.

Part I, on the knowledge base of practice, consists of (1) an interesting and useful typology of treatment and task groups; (2) an abbreviated and highly selective exposition of historical developments

© 1986 by The Haworth Press, Inc. All rights reserved.

in group work practice; (3) understanding of group dynamics, classified as communication and interaction patterns, group attraction, social control, and group culture; and stages or group development. It also includes knowledge about the professional worker as leader of the group with power attributed to him from several sources, who uses an interactional model of leadership and a set of skills for facilitating group processes, gathering data, making assessments, and taking action. The knowledge base is generic to both task and treatment groups and to varied models of practice. Other theoreticians, however, subscribe to a more extensive knowledge base that includes the nature and quality of interpersonal relationships and interpersonal, intragroup, and intergroup conflicts. They also view as essential, knowledge about the biological, psychological, and social growth and development of persons throughout the life cycle, personality dynamics with special reference to the coping and problem-solving capacities of the ego, and cultural factors as these influence individual or group functioning.

Part II consists of chapters on phases of group development, assessment, and evaluation. The material on planning incorporates contemporary knowledge concerning this important phase of practice. The succeeding chapters contain clear descriptions of the tasks of the worker. Although the introductory chapter placed emphasis on the group as the instrument of change and on balanced attention to socio-emotional needs and task accomplishments, these principles are not carried over into discussions of intervention. Likewise, although it was asserted that psychoanalytic theory has an important influence on group work practice, the formulations of assessment and treatment do not incorporate concepts from that body of knowledge. Almost no attention is given to the quality of the worker's relationships with individuals, subgroups, and the group as a whole, nor to member to member relationships. The authors do not explain why this is so.

The generic activities of the worker in treatment groups are described as preparing for meetings, structuring the work, achieving contracted behaviorally specific goals, and monitoring and evaluating progress. Primary attention is given to the use of a large repertoire of behavioral and physical activities as varied as sculpting, flooding, modeling, role playing, progressive muscle relaxation, bioenergetics, rolling, contingency management, systematic desensitization, and hypnosis. The different theoretical orientations from which these procedures were developed are not discussed, nor are there cautions about the possible dangers in the use of some of these techniques. The worker's actions are directive, behaviorally specific, highly structured, and individual-oriented. There are no illustrations of the use of group process in planning and conducting them. The worker is clearly the powerful agent of change.

In addition to direct work with individuals in the context of the group, attention is given to changing group processes and environmental conditions and policies that have a bearing on individual and group functioning.

The chapter on intervention with task groups in the middle phase of group development is a major contribution to the literature on social work practice. Decision-making, free and open discussion of ideas, and problem-solving processes are given considerable attention. In several other models of social work with treatment groups, such processes are also used extensively (Somers, 1976), and it is not clear why Toseland and Rivas limit such knowledge to task groups. In general, the content on intervention with task groups is superior to that of treatment groups, perhaps because such groups are, by nature, more formally structured and task-centered.

Studies of models of practice indicate that, in spite of some important differences, there is a pervasive theme that knowledge about the structure, processes, and development of small groups is necessary for effective practice. The new book contains considerable generic knowledge about small groups as systems in environments. It is in ideas about change processes and interventions that theoretical and practical differences emerge. In spite of valiant efforts, the authors could not fulfill their purpose of integrating existing knowledge about the practice of group work. That would probably be an impossible task: many of the theoretical propositions that underlie varied models of practice seem to be incongruent.

The book has many outstanding features. It moves the profession ahead by its typologies of task and treatment groups and by describing the knowledge, processes, and skills that are generic to them. Its chapters on assessment and evaluation go beyond those in any other recent book on group work: they focus not only on content and outcome, but also on differential means for assessing and evaluating individuals and groups. There are excellent comparative analyses of important group structures and stages of group development. The chapter on planning deals more thoroughly with this subject than does any other book to date. The book is well organized, scholarly, and contains an excellent bibliography.

The authors refer to their model of intervention as an interactional one, the same term that William Schwartz used at times to typify his work. Toseland's and Rivas' logical positivist and highly structured behavioral approach to intervention should not, however, be confused with the humanistic, process-oriented, relationship, and mutual aid focus of Schwartz' orientation. Theoreticians who espouse process-oriented or psychodynamic views of practice can, nevertheless, learn much from reading this interesting book.

Helen Northen
Professor Emeritus
School of Social Work
University of Southern California

REFERENCE

Somers, Mary Louise. ''Problem-Solving in Small Groups,'' in Robert W. Roberts and Helen Northen. *Theories of Social Work with Groups.* New York: Columbia University Press, 1976.